MADEIRA & PORTO SANTO

Madeira & Porto Santo

CRISTINA LEITÃO

C. A. LEITÃO PUBLICATIONS
MADEIRA

CONTENTS

INTRODUCTION

THROUGHOUT THE AGES Madeira has been a rather well-kept secret. Out on the fringes of Europe, along with neighbouring islands in the group, it is a symbol of Portugal's extraordinary spirit of adventure. It was here that the voyages of discovery gained a new impulse, and became an important bridge between the New World and Europe.

For centuries the island was a strategic port of call due to its singular location. Set in the Atlantic Ocean nearly 1000 kilometres from Lisbon and 608 kilometres from the coast of Morocco, it was the ideal place for passing ships to stop off for provisions. Madeira's capital, Funchal, received a constant flow of travellers and traders who would settle here or stop briefly. It was this mix of cultures, ideas, and traditions and the constant exchange of goods that created the city as it stands today. Madeira is very cosmopolitan, yet remains fiercely true to its Portuguese heritage.

History

TO FULLY UNDERSTAND this island of contrasts, one has to follow its history. The origins of Madeira date back at least five million years, to the Miocene period when volcanic underwater eruptions exploded in the eastern Atlantic Ocean. These successive eruptions built layer upon layer of materials, which eventually emerged from the sea as an island – one of which was Madeira, the largest and most populated of the islands, Porto Santo, the only other populated island, and the Desertas and the Selvagens, both uninhabited sanctuaries harbouring endangered animal species. Madeira's volcanoes are now dormant, with the last eruption taking place six thousand years ago, although there are small manifestations in the form of hot pools and volcanic gases.

Madeira's warm climate must have been especially appealing during the Tertiary period, around fourteen thousand years ago when the rest of Europe was subjected to the massive freeze that destroyed all the laurel forests from the European continent. The island's relative isolation spared it from the destructive temperatures, and preserved those ancient forests which can still be seen high up on the mountains. Their unique presence has earned them classification as a Unesco world heritage site.

The islands remained unpopulated until the time João Gonçalvez Zarco officially discovered Madeira in 1419. Several expeditions must surely have passed the island as Greeks, Romans, Phoenicians, and Arabs all sailed the North Atlantic seas, but no trace of former occupation has ever been found. There is a reference to an *Insule de Lolegname*, an 'island of wood' on the well-known Genoese 'Medici map' which is dated 1351. However, the name may have been added after the Portuguese officially discovered the island: updating information on previously drawn maps was a fairly common practise.

It was not until 1419 that a group of young Portuguese explorers working for Prince Henry the Navigator stumbled on the island of Porto Santo and formalized its discovery. They were hurled there after a fearsome storm blew them off course while they where exploring the coast of Guinea. The island was named Porto Santo, or 'Sacred Port', and with the Prince's approval the explorers returned a year later to claim the other island they had seen in the distance, the island we know as Madeira.

Madeira's volcanic origins are stamped all over the landscape.

Madeira must have been a remarkable vision, a floating Eden in the middle of the Atlantic. It was immediately christened 'wood', due to the exuberant vegetation that covered the island. Records of the fifteenth century describe the wonderful dense forests, and how it was necessary to set fire to the giant trees so they could cultivate and build on the island. Gaspar Frutuoso, writing at this time, mentions a fire that raged for seven years and destroyed much of the island. This must be an exaggeration as we still find forests over a thousand years old in various parts of the island, but it does hint at the magnitude of the fires.

The enormous size of the trees empowered the Portuguese to build higher, sturdier masts on their *caravelas* or sailing ships, an improvement that eventually helped them to reach India. Even the buildings in mainland Portugal were improved as the beams made from the trunks could support the taller Moorish style houses.

The first boy and girl to be born in Madeira were christened Adam and Eve, which shows how the Portuguese were conscious that they were truly pioneers in a new world!

The influence of these first settlers is still present on the islands today.
Prince Henry the Navigator defined Madeira's future economy by introducing the Malvoisie vine from Crete and sugarcane from Sicily. Over the centuries the island's fortunes have varied dramatically. There were extreme highs as commerce in cane sugar and wine conquered the global stage. Later, terrible lows were suffered when the competition from new colonies wiped out Madeira's domination of the sugar market and devastating plagues all but eliminated the wine trade.

Prince Henry divided Madeira into three provinces: Tristão Vaz, a former soldier in Africa and one of the Prince's lieutenants received the eastern part of the island with its centre in Machico; João Gonçalves Zarco, a courageous nobleman who fought tirelessly for Prince Henry in Tangier, received the western part with Funchal at its centre; and Porto Santo was given to Bartolomeu Perestrelo, an Italian working for the Portuguese crown. The division lasted until the time of the Spanish occupation in 1580 when a single governor was appointed for the whole territory. The Spanish departed in 1640, but the divisions have stayed in place to this day.

Azulejos from the Casa-Museu Frederico de Freitas tile collection.

Sugarcane quickly dominated the economy, and by the end of the fifteenth century Madeira was the biggest sugar producer in Europe. The lucrative trade attracted merchants from all over the continent, and even Christopher Columbus visited the island to buy sugar. He left with more than he bargained for as he fell in love and married Filipa Perestrelo, daughter of the first governor of Porto Santo. Much of this episode in Columbus's life is hazy, but they did have a child and Filipa died shortly after. A little house in Porto Santo has been transformed into a Columbus museum as many believe he may have lived there at some point.

During this prosperous sugar phase, King D. Manuel took a personal interest in the planning of Funchal, ordering construction of the main buildings including a great church that would become the Sé Cathedral.

As the Azores and Brazil overtook Madeira as the main sugar exporters, the island was somewhat forgotten. Lack of attention from the Portuguese crown led to a demoralising attack in 1566 by French corsairs who looted the city and most of its treasures. As the city was virtually undefended, Bertrand de Montluc, a French pirate and his squadron of ships met virtually no resistance when they occupied the island for fifteen days. They killed hundreds of people and pillaged most of the churches. It was during this episode that the nuns of the Santa Clara convent fled in a procession to an isolated valley fifteen kilometres away. Today the valley, Curral das Freiras, is still named after them.

Pirates kept the inhabitants of Madeira and Porto Santo under a state of constant siege. Porto Santo suffered most, hit by successive attacks from the fifteenth to the eighteenth century. The population had to flee to the hills to escape the onslaughts by Algerian and Moorish corsairs and later the French and English brigands. The ruinous Montluc attack in the mid-sixteenth century changed the way the island was governed, forcing high-level Portuguese officials to live permanently on the island and strengthen Funchal's military defences.

A sea of clay tile roofs complement Funchal's historical buildings. Tower of the Santa Clara convent (above right).

Madeira wine flourished during the seventeenth century, outpacing sugarcane as the mainstay of the economy. It was at this time that the British presence on the island began to increase, influenced by the marriage of Catherine of Braganza to Charles II of England. During the wedding negotiations the Queen Regent Luisa of Portugal actually considered including Madeira in Catherine's dowry, ceding it to England together with Tangier and Bombay. Legend has it that a Madeiran scribe drew up the treaty and deliberately forgot to mention the islands. One result of this alliance was that Madeira was not included in the protectionist ban on products exported from Europe to the British colonies. This led to many British merchants settling in Madeira so they could export wine from the island to the Americas.

Throughout the eighteenth century Madeira was strategically placed at the centre of the most important trade routes. The English fleets sailed by on their way to the West Indies as did many European scientists and explorers. Captain Cook passed by twice in 1768 and 1772, and Charles Darwin visited the island several times. In *The Origin of the Species* he mentions more animal species from Madeira than from the Galapagos Islands.

During the Napoleonic Wars, Madeira twice endured a benevolent occupation by the British forces. They came the first time without warning their oldest ally, and this led to a diplomatic incident. Their official aim was to protect the island as it was a vital port for the English navy and the threat of French attacks was imminent. The occupying force arrived in 1801, followed by a second invasion in 1807 under the command of General William Carr Beresford that lasted until 1814, at the end of the war with France.

When Napoleon was being taken into exile on the HMS Northumberland, the ship anchored in Funchal harbour on the 23 August 1815 to stock up on wine amongst other things. The only person allowed on board during this time was Henry Veitch, the British Consul. He was later removed from his post for addressing Napoleon as 'Your Majesty' and not 'General' as he had been instructed. According to legend, some of the wine left by Napoleon was returned to the island. It was supposedly bottled in 1840 by Blandy's, one of the oldest British companies on the island and later served to Winston Churchill at the Reid's Hotel.

'Un doigt de vin de Madere anima les regards, fit sourire les levres'

ANATOLE FRANCE, *Le Petit Pierre* (1844-1924)

In the nineteenth century, Russia became the principal market for Madeira wine, with the Grand Duke ordering some 76 000 cases a year. After two severe outbreaks of disease pest attacked the vines, *Oidium Tuckeri*, also known as powdery mildew, in the 1850s and *Phylloxera Vastatrix*, the vine louse, during the 1870s, most of the wine firms went out of business and it looked for a while as though the Madeira wine industry was at an end. By the next decade they had the pests under control, but already port and sherry had superseded Madeira in the wine market.

Madeira was one of the first true tourism destinations, becoming a fashionable stopping point for the European aristocracy and intelligentsia throughout the nineteenth and twentieth century. The island's unique therapeutic and scenic qualities attracted many people looking for a recovery from tuberculosis. The Portuguese writer Julio Dinis, who came to the island to convalesce from 1869 to 1871, described the numerous foreigners who could be found wandering the streets, among them Germans, Brazilians, North Americans, Russians, and English. Generally the convalescents found the atmosphere on the island to be romantically melancholic rather than morbid or depressing.

Among the visiting aristocracy, Queen Adelaide of England came in 1850, and the tragic Austro-Hungarian Empress Sissi also stayed on the island several times and recalled her happy days here. In 1901 there was great excitement as Funchal became the temporary residence of the Portuguese kings. This was a momentous event as none had ever made a formal visit to the island. Fantastic celebrations were held, and there are still people alive who remember their parents describing how the trees around the cathedral were lit with candles as the Queen went to mass.

Karl I the last emperor of Austria died in Madeira soon after he was exiled here in 1921. He is buried at the Igreja do Monte.

During the First World War, Germany declared war on Portugal, and on the 3rd December 1916 a German U-boat that had been hiding in a cove around Ponta de São Lourenço emerged to sink a French warship, *La Surprise*, and two other ships anchored in the bay of Funchal. It also shelled the town, slightly damaging the Santa Clara convent, wounding the priest as he celebrated mass, and killing two congregants.

The impact of the Second World War was felt on the island even though Portugal remained neutral. With virtually no supplies reaching Madeira, there was a sharp fall in the number of tourists. Portugal became a Republic in 1910, and soon fell under the dictatorship of Salazar. His regime lasted for thirty five years. Madeira was severely disciplined following the 1931 revolt provoked by the 'Hunger Law.' The unrest was inflamed by the monopoly on imported flour held by a small group of mill owners. This was followed by a general strike, and the workers then attacked the mills. The response from Salazar was crushing, and soon the culprits were rounded up and deported to the Azores and Cape Verde.

The Portuguese revolution in 1974 signalled a new rise in the island's fortunes, with Madeira given the status of an Autonomous Political Region. Alberto João Jardim was elected President of the regional government in 1976 for the Social Democratic Party, and has won every election for the past twenty-eight years. His popularity is due both to his charismatic qualities as a leader and to the staggering growth in the island's economy in the last quarter century.

Madeira has re-invented itself from a deprived, isolated, agricultural region to one of the most attractive destinations in Europe. Tourism is now the pearl in the island's economy, with the emphasis on four and five star quality hotels and ecotourism. A free trade zone has also boosted international investment. Madeira has gained the title of 'Europe's Internet Capital', with the largest service providers now setting camp in Funchal just as the British wine merchants did in the seventeenth century.

The seventeenth century S. Tiago Fortress.

Funchal

NOTHING QUITE PREPARES one for the spectacular sight of Funchal surrounded by mountains. The blue sea sparkles in the distance and the rolling cluster of houses and gardens spreads around the valley.

From the time the Portuguese explorer João Gonçalves Zarco arrived in 1420 and named the city after *funcho*, the fennel plant growing abundantly there, the breathtaking landscape and natural beauty of the bay have captivated visitors ever since.

A permanent subtropical climate guarantees deliciously warm temperatures year round, and yet the atmosphere is more like southern Europe than the tropics. Funchal is ablaze with colour, with vivid pink bougainvillea, purple Jacaranda and spectacular red Flame trees lining the main avenues, offering cool shade and a cheerful atmosphere.
The city rises around a natural amphitheatre above the sea, up to Pico do Areeiro at 1818 meters high, and covering an area of about 76 square kilometres. Although it is the third most densely populated city in Portugal one doesn't feel crowded as everything is built on the terraces that gracefully cover the valley. Gardens of every shape, size and variety adorn the city, giving the impression in a continuous flow of colour.

In the old quarter, the houses seem to have sprung up naturally from the earth. One neighbourhood, the Zona Velha (old town) in Santa Maria, is now a protected area displaying unique architecture. A labyrinth of ancient houses and narrow cobbled streets invite one to dive in and explore. Many date back to medieval times and the original ovens can still be seen jutting out from the walls. Artisans and craftsmen still practise skills like boot making or furniture restoration in their small workshops.

Over the past decade this area has been substantially restored in a formerly rough part of Funchal. It boasts an elegant new hotel called the Porto Santa Maria, good local restaurants and a sheltered garden where men gather to play cards each afternoon. Among the tiny houses stands the imposing S.Tiago Fortress, built early in the seventeenth century during the Spanish occupation which lasted from 1580 to 1640. It is now the Museum of Contemporary Art.

Funchal is a carpet of blues and greens. In the old quarter houses have stood firm for over four hundred years.

TISSOT

The Mercado dos Lavradores stands a short walk away. It was designed along Art Deco lines in the 1930s by Edmundo Tavares, a leading Portuguese architect. It opens on to a courtyard, bursting to life each morning when the fruit arrives from the local sellers and the flower stalls are filled with orchids, birds of paradise, and camellias. All sorts of tropical fruits are sold and can also be sampled. Above, on the first floor, the arcades surrounding the courtyard also sell fruit, spices, herbs and vegetables. At the far end lies the fish market, displaying dramatic looking fish including tuna, scabbard and many other varieties.

Each quarter of Funchal has its own personality, and as soon as one passes from the old part to the Sé district one can sense the change. The city is divided by three rivers, brilliantly covered with scarlet and purple bougainvillea climbing over trellises, the brainchild of a Frenchman, Brigadier Reynaldo Oudinot, who was hired to solve Funchal's flooding problems after the 1803 deluge which killed six hundred people.

'This lilliput of the tropics, for the rest, is more brilliant than if flowering in a hundred climates of its own'

SACHEVERELL SITWELL, *Portugal and Madeira* (1954)

Biscuits are still baked in the traditional way at Fabrica de Santo António, which has been in the same family for generations.

Funchal has been described as the most Portuguese of cities that rose during the period of the discoveries. King D. Manuel created his 'model city,' fashioning the most important buildings after examples of other Portuguese cities of the time. Funchal itself did not follow any grand plan, but simply grew up around the valley, expanding rapidly when the city's economy flourished with the sugar trade. The architecture in Funchal is mainly characterized by Gothic and Baroque buildings, dominated by solid and austere designs with elaborately decorated ceilings. Among the most distinctive ornamental features is the basalt around the windows and door frames. The older red variety made of volcanic tuff, dates back to the earliest settlement and was painted to stand the test of time. The grey basalt and the paler Porto Santo basalt that decorate most of the fine old buildings are of eighteenth century vintage.

The charming clay-tiled roofs add a romantic touch to the city with their 'Chinese Chippendale' look, a fashion that was all the rage in Portugal throughout the eighteenth and nineteenth centuries. This oriental influence can be seen in the upturned pointed curves and the corner motifs depicting dragons. The corner motifs also reveal delightful figures of doves, children, griffons, cats, and even British bulldogs. Pattern tiled floors can be seen gracing the terraces and courtyards with the most beautiful designs in different colours.

Several traditional shops and bakeries operate as they would have done half a century ago. The Fabrica Santo Antonio produces *broas de mel* (a cornbread sweetened with honey), and wonderful exotic jams, and the Pastelaria Lua in the Rua Carreira still makes the best Bolo Rei, a puff pastry ring decorated with dried fruits eaten around the New Years.

From patterned floors to intricate ceilings and roofs, discovering Funchal's architecture is a source of never-ending pleasure.

The people of Funchal are very sociable, forever stopping for a quick coffee and a fix on the latest gossip. A row of three *cafés* along the Avenida Arriaga are favourite haunts for meeting friends; the Café do Teatro set alongside the Municipal Theatre is the trendiest of the three. The Golden Gate Café, once nicknamed the 'corner of the world', is more traditional but still pulls in the leading lights of Madeiran society. Older folk meet at the Café do Apolo, just in front of the cathedral.

The city centre, the hub of Funchal revolves around the Sé Cathedral where all the original governing buildings have stood for five centuries. King D. Manuel commissioned the cathedral in 1485, giving meticulous orders on how the church should be constructed and paid for. It was built by Pero Annes who was described as the 'master carpenter of the work', and Gil Enes, the 'master stonemason of the Sé'. It was completed in 1514.
The ceiling is particularly beautiful. High above the aisle and both naves, it is made of ivory-coloured cedar wood inlaid in the Mudéjar style. The original baptismal font and wooden altar offered by King D. Manuel are still in use. The building has survived many heavy-handed interventions, but now science is playing a part in the work to restore the most important parts of the cathedral to their former glory.

If one uses the cathedral as a starting point, there are dozens of roads and squares to explore, all paved in the traditional cobblestones made popular by the Marques de Pombal who reconstructed Lisbon following the 1755 Lisbon earthquake. The cobblestone fashion spread to most Portuguese towns, each creating a unique design in black basalt and white limestone. Every kind of shop and small restaurant lines these streets.

The ceiling of the Sé Cathedral is decorated with intricate patterns carved out of wood in the neo-Islamic fashion of the early sixteenth century.

The Museu de Arte Sacra (Museum of Sacred Art) is set in the former bishops' palace. It dates back to 1600 and boasts eighteenth century *azulejos* (decorative tiles) on its verandas. The museum houses a wonderful collection of Flemish paintings bought at the height of the sugarcane trade in the sixteenth century by local merchants, often as payment. Among the most famous works are the paintings of Joos Van Cleve, Jan Provoost, and Dieric Bouts who was a pioneer in the drawing of perspective. Several religious artefacts are on display including a gilt processional cross given by King D. Manuel and a number of statues.

The museum stands on one side of the Praça do Municipio, an elegant square that is also fronted by the city hall and the Jesuit College. Open air concerts are performed here during the year beside the fountain designed by the Portuguese architect Raul Lino in 1942. The Jesuits came to Madeira immediately after the French corsair attack in 1566, checking to see if the local population had suffered any 'Protestant contamination'. After a welcoming stay, they went on to organize the Jesuit College which was completed in 1647. The Church is especially striking with one of the most important set of seventeeth century gilt carvings in Portugal, a lovely collection of *azulejos* from the seventeenth and eighteenth century, and Mudéjar inspired wall paintings. The Jesuits were expelled from the island in 1759 and all their property confiscated and put up for sale at public auction.

Flemish masterpieces at the Sacred Art Museum.

Café do Teatro, Marginal, and Café do Museu keep Funchal awake well into the early hours.

Up the hill past the Rua das Pretas, named after the African slave girls who would run up and down the road on errands from the fifteenth to the eighteenth century, the S. Pedro and Santa Clara area begins. This was where the most important families first settled, and also where the great Franciscan monastery and convent were built.

Climbing the very steep Calçada de Santa Clara road leads to the Casa-Museu Frederico de Freitas. Here a very eclectic collection of English and Portuguese furniture, paintings and carvings relating to Madeira are shown. The most impressive attraction is the annex which houses an invaluable collection of Portuguese, Persian, Moorish and Turkish *azulejos*. The house is a perfect example of a grand Funchal town house, complete with a charming *casinha de prazer*. These little gazebos were normally made of wood, surrounded by shutters or trellis, and set at the bottom of the garden overlooking the street. Ladies enjoyed them in the past century embroidering and having tea there while keeping a sharp eye on what was going on in the street. Rua Conde de Carvalhal and Rua Levada Sta. Luzia are excellent places to spot colourful examples of the summerhouses.

Further along, the Santa Clara Convent continues to carry out the same purpose it did five hundred year ago when João Gonçalves da Camâra, Zarco's son, founded it. He created the convent in 1497 and Zarco himself is buried under the altar. A nun will guide you round, showing the precious seventeenth century tiles with the famous Santa Clara pattern adorning the wall of the main church and the lovely Camellia tiles in the little chapel. The cloister has its original floors with extremely rare sixteenth century Mudéjar tiles from Seville, and each chair is decorated with a cherub. The convent was one of the few casualties of the First World War, when a German submarine bombarded the city from the bay and hit the main chapel, which was badly harmed, but since then has been completely restored.

Locally known as 'pleasure houses' these gazebos are the icing on the cake to the lovely Funchal gardens.

Across the road the Quinta das Cruzes museum was the home of Zarco, the first governor of Funchal. Set in a lovely property of about a hectare, the gardens have architectural relics rescued when old buildings were demolished. These include Manueline window frames, gargoyles, and tombstones. Inside the house there are impressive collections of silver, porcelain, English furniture and large wooden sugar packing cases.

Strolling back down the road to the Avenida Arriaga it is time for a drink and nowhere better than the Adegas de São Francisco, also known as the Old Blandy Wine Lodges. Originally a sixteenth century Franciscan monastery, it became a fitting place for the Madeira Wine Company to store its ageing wines, including most of the leading names such as Blandy's, Miles, Cossart Gordon and Leacock. The world of Madeira wine can be explored in these cellars, the vintage room alone housing hundreds of bottles, which are stored and ready for sale – in all there are 800 000 litres of wine stored in the cellars. The oldest surviving bottle of Madeira dates from 1715, and here one can buy the Cossart Gordon 1908 Bual. Upstairs the scent of cedar wood surrounding the vats is intoxicating as they reach their full maturity in a naturally warm environment.

Across the road stands the Palácio de São Lourenço, one of the finest examples of seventeenth century fortifications in Portugal, and just beyond it the charming Municipal Theatre, built between 1884 and 1887 was modelled on La Scala in Milan.

The Livraria Esperança (above) claims to have the largest bookstore in the country.

'The Câmara, built by that same Conde de Carvalhal who laid out Palheiro with so much taste, has an agreeable courtyard with an elegant staircase'

SUSAN LOWNDES, *The Selective Traveller in Portugal* (1958)

There is an impressive variety of places to stay in Funchal, for any pocket or taste. The Madeirans have developed hospitality to an art form, and nowhere else in Portugal is the service so good or standards so high. Reid's Palace Hotel is one of the finest on the island exuding the luxurious atmosphere of a bygone era. Built by the Scot, William Reid, who arrived on the island in 1836 at the age of fourteen, with £5 in his pocket, and who set about building his vision of the most luxurious hotel in Europe. Before long the hotel was *the* place to stay for the rich and fashionable. Empress Elizabeth I of Austria was among the first to sign the guest book, and later names added included George Bernard Shaw, Sir Winston Churchill, and King Umberto of Italy. The names of the guests have changed but the service and setting remains the same. Afternoon tea is still served on the balcony with a pyramid of scones, sandwiches, innumerable pastries, and Reid's special blend of Twinings tea.

Reid's is one of the more fascinating hotels of the Orient Express chain, with superb gardens and offering exceptional comfort.

'... Empress Elizabeth I of Austria was among the first to sign the guest book, and later names included George Bernard Shaw, Sir Winston Churchill, and King Umberto of Italy ...'

Porto Bay

Next door, the view from the Cliff Bay is equally inspiring, a perfect blue sea with ships dotting the horizon. Rows of deckchairs near the large pool area below provide a perfect sunbathing experience. The French chef is one of the best on the island, creating exquisite dishes which look as beautiful as they taste.

Even a four star hotel such as the new Vila Porto Mare in the Lido area matches the five star quality of furnishings and service, with spa and cuisine to match.

Oscar Niemeyer, the Brazilian architect who designed Brasilia, also created the Casino da Madeira in the 1970s with a conference hotel beside it in the shape of a sun and moon. An extensive hotel area has developed along the Estrada Monumental with numerous five star and four star hotels lining the coastline. Tourism is the driving force behind Madeira's prosperity and it shows in the welcoming way visitors are treated. For those more interested in a natural setting, there are country house hotels set in historic *quintas,* or new ventures such as the stylish Choupana Hills Resort, an Asian inspired hotel with opulent bungalows on stilts set high in the hills overlooking Funchal.

The Cliff Bay has cultivated the art of hospitality to perfection.

Further up the mountains that surround Funchal lies Monte village, some six hundred meters above sea level. Each year on August 15 the largest religious procession on the island takes place at the twin towered church of Nossa Senhora do Monte, where the exiled Emperor Karl I of Austria is buried. The famous sleds stationed just below the church on the mountainside, offer a thrilling ride down the hill as the white-clad men who handle them spend a fair amount of their time drinking in the bar next door. Hemingway described the experience as 'one of the most exhilarating in all my life', which goes to show he too must have been under the influence ...

The European aristocracy in the nineteenth century flocked to Monte to recover from tuberculosis, renting the *quintas* or country houses that were enhanced by beautiful gardens. The *quintas* in Madeira are simpler and more austere in architecture than their mainland counterparts, but compensated by the sumptuous landscaping.

Maria Lamas, the Portuguese writer described how fabulous these *quintas* were in their prime. Regrettably very few survive as they did a century ago. The splendid Quinta do Til, owned today by a local businessman was famous for the giant Madeira Laurel tree that grew over 50 metres high and was the reference point for boats reaching Funchal bay. The house also held a morbid attraction for visitors as the only son of George Canning, the British prime minister, was drowned in the garden tank, and in the twentieth century a fire destroyed most of the house and the priceless porcelain collection. The Count of Canavial, a talented doctor and superb host, built the Quinta Canavial with miniature replicas of the Versailles fountains and the first ice-skating ring in Madeira and enjoyed cultivating silk worms there. Besides the country estates in Funchal, there are also handsome *quintas* in Jardim da Serra, Camacha, Santo da Serra and on the island's northern coast.

The hamlet of Curral das Freiras, named for the nuns who fled from rapacious pirates to the pine-forested valley in the sixteenth century remained secluded until a road constructed in 1959 connected the village to the outside world. The walks around here are fragrant with the scent of wildflowers; ferns lining the paths, and the views from Eira do Serrado (1095 meters above sea level) make the steep climb worthwhile.

Exploring the Island

HOWEVER MUCH FUNCHAL enchants one with its many delights, there is always a pressing curiosity to set off on a discovery of the island. Madeira is bursting with diversity; the landscape offers so many choice of scenery, with the mountains, sea and gardens all bringing about a vision of complete beauty.

The best way to explore Madeira is to cover the eastern side, then move inland and north-west, and finally tour the western coast.

The Eastern coastline

This side takes us back along the coastline to the charming village of Santa Cruz just near the airport. Santa Cruz is a little town rich in history that dates back to the time of the first settlement. The elegant Manueline church, built in 1533, has graceful gothic arches and pillars and invites a look inside. The town itself deserves a visit even if just to sip a *brisa maracuja* (a local soft drink made of passion fruit) at the Palmeira restaurant, with its strategic location right on the sea it's the perfect place to spot planes passing right in front just seconds before landing. There is a good fruit and fish market supplied by local fishermen who draw their colourful boats up to the shingle beach just beyond the market.

Further along the road past the airport Machico springs to view, this is where explorers João Gonçalves Zarco and Tristão Vaz first landed on Madeira. It became the second most important town, later governed by Tristão Vaz. Legend has it that the city is named after Robert Machim, whose tragic love story dates back to the fourteenth century before the island was officially discovered. The story goes that the English Anne d'Arfet and Robert Machim fell madly in love, and to prevent this unsuitable match her family immediately married her off to some suitor and had Robert imprisoned. This was no deterrent to Robert Machim as he smuggled Anne out of her house and they both eloped on his boat from Bristol. They finally ended up marooned on Madeira, were Anne and then Robert died after being abandoned there by some of the crew. Zarco found the two graves and named the settlement in their honour. Whether or not this romantic name origin is correct, Machico does have a slightly melancholic aura. The centre of the city is built around the main square, the Largo do Município, where the fifteenth century parish church is situated. Designed in the Manueline style, it has a wonderful gothic portal offered by King D. Manuel to the wife of Tristão Vaz. Machico is still an important fishing port, and the nineteenth century fish market is vibrant. At Pico do Facho men kept a vigilant watch for pirates. Usually Porto Santo Island would light a bonfire. This alerted the lookouts in Machico, and they would then light their bonfire, in turn warning the Garajau lookout, a message finally passed on to Funchal. This ingenious alarm system gave the cities a couple of hours to prepare for the oncoming pirate attack.

The Gulf Stream warms the coastal waters around the island making swimming a pleasure year-round.

A winding road up the hill and through the tunnel leads to the sleepy village of Caniçal. This is a true fishing village from which men leave their families for months at a time to trawl the deep Atlantic waters and along the coast of Africa. Caniçal was a whaling centre for a couple of decades, a profitable trade launched by an Azorean in the beginning of the twentieth century. When the sentinels spotted whales from Pico do Facho they sounded the alert, and took off in their tiny open boats to battle with the great whales. Gregory Peck and John Huston came to Madeira to film Moby Dick in the 1950's and their party killed twenty whales in a single outing. The whaling finally ended in 1981 with an international ban on whale hunting, and the waters around Madeira are now a protected marine mammal sanctuary. Caniçal had been completely isolated from the rest of the island up until the time a tunnel was built in the 1950's from Machico to Caniçal. Before then, a sea journey was the only way to go to or from the small village. Since initiating Madeira as a Free Trade Zone, a yacht marina has been built and plans are also underway for a luxurious hotel resort in the area. For visitors who enjoy the fishing village ambience, their trip will be enhanced by lunching or dining at one of the restaurants near the water and sampling the *castanhetas (Chromis chromis)* small fried flat fish served with octopus or limpet rice. To bring the meal to perfection, those in the know choose Coral, a highly successful locally-brewed beer.

Halt for a while between Canical and Ponta de S. Lourenco at Prainha, the only black sandy beach on the island. There is a haunting beauty at Ponta de S. Lourenço with its desolate scenery and the lonely windmills turning on the horizon. When Zarco first arrived on this easternmost point of the island, he christened it after his ship, the S. Lourenco. Unlike anywhere else on the island, one sees no trees, but walking amidst the wildflowers growing on the hillsides, one spots the places were roots of an ancient petrified forest once grew. The landscape is breathtaking, with imposing views of the plunging cliffs and rough waters below.

Dragon trees in Santa Cruz (left). The barren landscape at Ponta de S. Lourenço is a dramatic change from the rest of the island (above).

Returning past Machico, a tire-squealing climb on a road lined with hydrangea and agapanthus, the ride comes to a halt at Santo da Serra. Mimosas flower in spring along the roadside, and the village is known for its especially beautiful camellias. The climate around here is alpine, mindful of a Northern European town complete with chilly weather and mist. Perhaps this is why so many homesick English families chose Santo as their second home during the eighteenth and nineteenth centuries. Even the country houses, complete with stables and formal gardens, seem to recreate the English countryside and act as a cool escape from stuffy summer days in Funchal.

The Santo da Serra golf course has been described as one of the most beautiful courses in the world. This was where golf first took hold on the island in 1933 with a handful of members playing on the mountainous 9-hole course. Nowadays there is a 27-hole course that is kept in mint condition as it prepares for the annual Madeira Island Open held each year at Santo around March. Champion golfer

Seve Ballesteros is a fan, and it is easy to see why. With its 360º views of mountains, sparkling ocean and Porto Santo Island in the distance it is a wonder anyone plays golf at all as the view is such a wonderful diversion. An interesting volcanic crater nearby is filled with water that supplies the village and golf course.

Quinta do Santo is worth a call, here one can walk in the gardens and see the acid soil plants that thrive in this region – a variety of rhododendrons, azaleas and camellias.

From Santo da Serra an inland road eventually winds down to the village of Camacha. The main attraction here is the wicker industry, this seems to have stopped in time as they still churn out the same chairs, baskets and figures they did a hundred years ago. Camacha is also famous for its many folklore groups, and also for the camellia lined quintas built at a cool 700 metres above sea level. Apparently it was here that football was first introduced on the island by Harry Hinton in 1875, and then rapidly became the number one sport in Madeira.

Machico has kept most of its architectural heritage intact, with a manueline church dating from the time of the first settlers and a 1706 fortress gracing the city.

Inland and Northeast

To explore the northeast coast takes at the very least a whole day. Prepare by choosing an onion-style approach to dressing, with various layers of clothing, as it is quite normal during this drive to move into several different microclimates from one minute to the next, with a thick mist suddenly opening onto a brilliant sunny day.

One way to reach the northeast coast is to drive inland, up past Monte and Terreiro da Luta, through Pico do Areeiro and Ribeiro Frio, and down to Santana and Ponta Delgada.

After climbing to 1400 metres but before reaching Pico do Areeiro, Poiso is an excellent place to stop for a coffee. The restaurant *Abrigo do Poiso* used to be the government shelter where rain-battered travellers crossing the mountains could seek some warmth. The *poncha* – a typical drink made with very strong *aguardente*, lemons and sugar, is legendary here. One of the most overwhelming sights in Madeira is the view from Pico do Areeiro. Rising majestically 1818 metres above sea level, the panorama takes one very far from the popular postcard image Madeira. Here the mountain range commands respect, a real life Mount Olympus that on a sunny day captures a unique picture of the mountain tops rising from a sea of clouds.

Ribeiro Frio is set deep within an ancient forest, and is a perfect starting point to learn about Madeira's Laurel forest. Water gushes from the waterfalls, passing through to the agricultural terraces that cover the surrounding valleys. A trout hatchery marks another *poncha* Mecca called Victor's Bar, which tends to have too many tour buses for comfort, though on a quiet day it's a good place to stop for a bite.

The distinctive features along the coastline, like the emerald green valleys and amusing little villages that pop up from nowhere, make the drive along the northeast coast a surprising delight. A hundred or so thatched triangular houses have made Santana a favourite with visitors. These curious dwellings have existed on the island since the sixteenth century, but the oldest remaining examples are about one hundred years old. The simple design consists of two A-shaped wooden frames that hold the hut up, with colourful doors and windows and the interior divided into an upstairs sleeping quarter and downstairs living area.

The whole area around Santana, São Jorge and Boaventura is rolling with vineyards. The road to São Jorge from Santana is lined with arum and bugle lilies. Quinta do Furão stands in a privileged spot high on a cliff overlooking the sea. The best time to come to this hotel and restaurant is during the grape-picking season in September, when one can help out with the grape crushing. One of the most memorable experiences is to wake up at the Quinta do Arco

de São Jorge, walk outside ones wood cabin with a coffee and see the extraordinary wall of mountains in front. This *Quinta* is set to become the largest rose garden in the Iberian Peninsula, with over seventeen thousand roses of one thousand varieties planted. The little seaside hamlet of Arco de São Jorge, is surrounded by an arch (hence the name *arco*), which was caused by a massive landslide thousands of years ago. This region is well known for producing delicious organic crops, mainly grapes as the land is exceptionally fertile.

17 000 roses grow at Quinta do Arco de São Jorge, a magical complement to the huge arch of mountains behind.

The Northwest

To the northwest of the island, São Vicente is a town standing at the bottom of a huge V-shaped valley where the long tunnel from Ribeira Brava emerges. This marks the place where the São Vicente caves are found, and is also the starting point of the coastal road to Porto Moniz.

The scenery along this coastal route, which is in fact a mere ledge, is a contrast of rock-breaking waves and waterfalls that cascade down from the cliffs above. Even with the threat of breakaway rocks falling onto the car or being splashed by ocean spray, the satisfaction one gets on having made it along this 19 kilometre road to the other side is well worth the adrenaline rush.

A stop at the Chão da Ribeira restaurant above Seixal is highly recommended before reaching the more crowded spots in Porto Moniz. Here a brilliant no fuss menu offers a choice of only two dishes: home grown trout or *espetada*. Both are delicious and arrive accompanied with limpet rice (made with the local sea animals with shells) or sizzling fried maize, potatoes and salad.

The name of Porto Moniz is associated with its natural rock pools, but apart from these there is little else to take your time. After a breathtaking ride to reach this town the immediate though is, now how do I get back? Locals in the village strongly recommend taking the upward drive past Paul da Serra where one can admire the neatly arranged agricultural plots and vineyards protected from the salty sea air by a curtain of tree heather. Reaching Paul da Serra one is again reminded that Madeira is truly an island of contrasts for up here a totally flat, lunar landscape stretches out for just under 20 kilometres. The plateau stands at a height of about 1500 meters and has an eerie magical quality to it, perhaps due to the sudden mists that descend on the plateau and the fact that it is totally uninhabited.

Nature is present everywhere in Rabaçal. Waterfalls plunge against the volcanic rocks bringing pure freezing water down to the streams that feed the stream channels. The mountains are covered in thick tree heathers that offer a shaded walk and disguise the height of the plunging ravines below.

Agriculture has blended naturally into the landscape all along the north coast.

FN1600 L
POPEY
D13928F

Discovering the Western Coast

The old coastal road dates from the nineteenth century and leads from Funchal to the small fishing village of Câmara de Lobos. This sunny region is mostly banana and vine territory. Zarco named the town 'chamber of wolves', because of the many sea lions sunbathing nosily on the beach. He organized the first settlement on Madeira here in 1420 as they waited for the raging fires they had lit in Funchal to subside so they could move in and cultivate the impossibly dense woodland.

Most of the scabbard fish served on the island are caught by the fishermen of Câmara de Lobos, their brightly coloured fishing boats piled high against each other along the beach. The boats come in different shapes and sizes, according to their use. Those taken out for scabbard are known as *espadeiros*, the red buoys inside them are used to signal where the kilometre long nylon line has been dropped. Pieces of squid are used on the end as bait. At night a spectacular sight is visible as all the buoys' lanterns flicker on the water.

Câmara de Lobos, one of Winston Churchill's favourite painting subjects.

In Estreito da Câmara de Lobos, the vineyards produce a fragrant wine, and the area is also filled with chestnut trees. In nearby Jardim da Serra there is a popular cherry festival every year in June. The cherries are small and pale, yet they taste so sweet and natural that they outshine their plumper foreign cousins. While most places on the island have *espetada* among the meat choices on the menu, Estreito is the rightful king. Here the meat tastes better, smells smokier and seems to slice like butter. Any good restaurant in Estreito will serve the laurel skewers hanging over each table where the custom is to slide the cube of meat down from the skewer with two forks. This is all enjoyed with good Portuguese red wine, triangles of garlic-buttered *bolo do caco* and mouth watering fried maize.

One of the highest sea cliffs in the world lies to the west of Câmara de Lobos. At 630 metres above sea level Cabo Girão offers spectacular views of the sea and of tiny patches of remote cultivated lands below.

To really appreciate the art of living in Madeira, you must head to Fajã dos Padres by boat (forty five minute boat ride) and spend the day there sunbathing and swimming in the pure waters. Fajã dos Padres, a little oasis created long ago by a landslide, once belonged to the Jesuit priests were they cultivated the land. Nowadays it can only be reached by boat or by a James Bond style elevator that hugs the cliff side. The cove has a tropical fruit plantation, a restaurant, and harbour. Lunch is a feast of local fish such as *castanhetas, chicharros* and tuna and one of the most heavenly puddings imaginable the *pitanga* cheesecake with fruit from the plantation.

Past the coastal town of Ribeira Brava the road skims along the seaside to Ponta do Sol. Here the village is built ingeniously against the mountainside with narrow steps darting to and from the houses. There is an excellent place to stay here: the Estalagem da Ponta do Sol. An elegantly designed hotel perched high on a cliff, it catches the peaceful atmosphere of this sleepy town in great style. The exquisite sunsets that lend their name to the village are best seen from the small bars near the waterfront, sipping a beer and savouring a *picadinho* – an appetiser of small chunks of meat in a delicious sauce which are speared with toothpicks and accompanied by chips.

Further along the coast lies the village of Madalena do Mar (Madeleine of the sea) founded by the exiled Henrique Alemão, so called because the locals couldn t understand his strange language. Some historians have claimed that this Henry the German who lived here in the fifteenth century, was in fact Ladsilau III, King of Poland and Hungary. After having lost a disastrous battle in 1444 the king disappeared and was never seen again. It is said that King D. João I offered him the chance to live in anonymity on the recently discovered Madeira Island. On one of his regular visits to see the governor Zarco, Henrique was recognized by two polish friars who had been sent to Madeira to beg him to return. Just as this mystery was about to be solved, Henrique was drowned when his ship sank after being hit by falling rocks near Cabo Girão. His son, trying to establish his father's true identity, was also drowned later on with all the proof he was bringing back to the family. Recently discovered letters in Germany seem to confirm that Ladislau III was indeed living in Madalena do Mar. The isolated village with such a noble history is nowadays a great banana and sugar cane producer.

The coastal road continues to Calheta, Jardim do Mar and Paul do Mar. The Manueline church in Calheta called Espirito Santo, has a fabulous Mudejar ceiling with intricate patterns and an ebony sacrarium offered by King D. Manuel I 'the fortunate' (1495–1521). A new contemporary art museum is nearly finished which will offer the most sophisticated exhibition centre to date on the island. Ponta do Pargo is the westernmost point of the island and one can head forward to Porto Moniz or turn upwards to Paul da Serra.

Quinta das Vinhas has restored most of its original 1685 features to create a perfect haven in Calheta.

Nature & Wildlife

ONE OF THE great fascinations of Madeira to visiting writers such as Sacheverell Sitwell, was that compared to other European islands it hardly had a past. This is true up to a point as there are no classical ruins or medieval buildings to admire, but there is a pre-historic forest that outlived the last ice age which wiped out the other laurel forests of Europe. Already in 1949, Susan Lowndes wrote in *The Selective Traveller* in Portugal that Madeira's true interest lay in the vegetation found here, the many species closely resembling European ones that are now extinct, but found in fossil rocks on the Continent, having survived in their isolation. Madeira has some of the best preserved vegetation remaining in the Makaronesia, as well as a long history of species introduced from all over the world.

The native flora of Madeira is what botanists call Palaearctic, which is normally found in northwest Europe, and was brought here by winds, visiting birds, or ocean currents. There are over one hundred and twenty plant species peculiar to the island that can't be found anywhere else in the world. One of these is the Madeira goodyera *(Goodyera macrophylla)*, an extremely fragile orchid, with white petals that grow at elevations between three hundred and eight hundred meters, with blooms measuring about 20–40cm.

In this relatively small island of 737 square kilometres, one can find several micro-climates, a chain of volcanic mountains that condenses the moist Atlantic air, sending water crashing into the pools below, and down by the sea, fertile coastal lands, basking in the steadily mild temperatures. The soils are acidic, poor in calcium and potassium but rich in humus.

Intact and unconquered, much of Madeira remains the same as it did thousands of years ago.

Laurel Forest of Madeira

The Laurisilva of Madeira is an outstanding relict of a previously widespread laurel forest–listed by UNESCO in 1999 as a world heritage site. It is the largest surviving area of laurel forest in the world, with enormous biological diversity. Nearly all its plants and animals are unique to the laurel forest, including many endemic animal species such as the Madeiran long-toed pigeon. This evergreen forest once covered 60% of the island, although nowadays it is probably no more than 20% but still with an area of over fifteen hundred hectares, mainly on the North coast.

Temperature is the crucial factor in determining where the forest is found, thriving in deep humid ravines such as Ribeiro Frio and Ribeiro da Janela where coastal fogs are common, and humidity levels reach well over 80%.
The forest is named after the predominant specie, the laurel *(Laurus azorica)*, which grows on the island at elevations between 300 and 1300 metres. The Madeira laurel *(Octoea foetens)*, Canary laurel *(Apollonias barbujana)*, Madeira mahogany *(Persea indica)*, and wax myrtle *(Myrica faia)* can also be found there forming a dense clump. Smaller trees such as the lily-of-the-valley tree *(Clethra arborea)*, Madeira cheesewood *(Pittosporum coriaceum)*, picconia *(Picconia excelsia)*, Madeira elder *(Sambucus lanceolata)* also thrive in this forest. Ferns, lichens and moss cover the ground below.

These forests are vital to the islands economy and hydrology, without them rivers of torrential water, rocks and mud would crash down the mountains to the lands below. They also produce an abundant flow of water, captured from the fogs that constantly surround the Laurisilva, filling the levadas – irrigation canals, and keeping the plantations well irrigated.

Above the 1300 metres where the Laurisilva ends, a completely different sort of vegetation grows, mainly small shrubs and very resistant heathers, immune to the cold and heavy rainfall.

Madeira's ancient laurel forests are a living relict of the last ice-age.

Wildlife

The only land mammals found here when the first settlers arrived were bats – eight species of them – this didn't put Charles Darwin off. He was truly impressed by Madeira's diverse insect species and their evolution. Currently there are 3300 species of invertebrates listed, mostly microscopic insects and snails, but according to biologists a continuous study would lead to thousands more being discovered.

In the Madeiran archipelago there are forty two known bird species, nine of which are unique to Madeira which has two of the largest bird sanctuaries in the world, the Desertas and the Selvagens.

Europe's rarest breeding bird the Zino's Petrel *(Pterodroma madeira)*, was re-discovered in Madeira in 1969, after it had been considered extinct, through the efforts of Alec Zino a local ornithologist. Together with his studies and DNA evidence they established that these birds were smaller and thinner-billed than the Bugio birds, which led to this tiny colony being confirmed as a separate species which is now known as Zino's Petrel. This small black and white seabird breeds in the high central mountains of the island and there are currently some forty-five mating pairs of them

The rare Long-toed-Pigeon or Madeira Laurel Pigeon *(Columba trocaz)* can only be found in Madeira, in the laurel forest. Perhaps 10 300 of these pigeons remain. Other birds include the White-faced Storm-petrel *(Pelagodroma marina hypoleuca)*, Madeiran Chaffinch *(Fringilla coelebs maderensis)*, Madeiran Firecrest *(Regulus ignicapillus madeirensis)*, and Spectacled Warbler *(Sylvia conspicillata orbitalis)*.

Amphibians and reptiles are scarce in number, but most of Funchal's gardens are crawling with friendly lizards such as the Madeiran wall lizard *(Teira dugesii dugesii)*.

The Desertas and the Selvagens are the two largest seabird sanctuaries in the world.

Although mammals are rare, there is a famous seal, the rarest in the world known as the Mediterranean monk seal *(Monachus monachus)*. In the wild there are only about five hundred seals, and twenty-three of these live in the Deserta Islands were they are protected, with guards making sure they are not disturbed. Spotted and blue dolphins are a common sight, and there are at least eighteen whale species in the surrounding waters.

Garajau, to the East of Funchal, has the only protected marine reserve in Portugal covering an area of over 376 hectares. Giant Dusky Groupers *(Epinephelus marginatus)* abound in the so-called 'valley of the meros', Mediterranean moray eels *(Muraena helena)*, Garden eels *(Heteroconger longissimus)*, Small devil rays *(Mobula mobular)* and Loggerhead turtles *(Caretta caretta)* can be found here, and it is an excellent place to scuba dive as the water is crystal clear and there are plenty of fish to be seen.

Madeira is famous among an exclusive group of world-class fishermen as one of the best places to catch a record breaking Blue marlin or Big eye tuna, with the average Blue marlin weighing over 700 lb. From May to September private boats and planes arrive in Madeira, and stay for several months at a time exclusively to fish in these deep Atlantic waters, filled with all sorts of record size species – Madeira has won the prestigious 4th of July Blue-Marlin fishing competition three times. Among the various big game fish found here are the Blue and White Marlin, Spearfish, Albacore, Dorado and Wahoo. Most of the big game fishermen here practice the 'tag and release' system, sending back the Blue Marlins into the ocean. One of the most exciting experiences is to go on a big game fishing boat here, with an excellent captain, such as Anibal of the Balancal and try your luck. Patience is essential, but well worth it for the unforgettable moments that come with catching a beautiful blue marlin.

The fabulously rich seas of Madeira are one of the best kept secrets of the islands.

Gardens of Madeira

MADEIRA IS RENOWNED for its fabulous gardens, with the glittering blue sea and mountain views acting as backdrops to complement the gardens always bursting with plants, flowers and a wonderful variety of trees.

The weather is temperate with a sub-tropical climate that makes it possible to grow plants from all over the world side-by-side. The rich volcanic soil creates an ideal base for them to flourish rapidly. All year long gardens are in bloom, and the fragrant scent of flowers and petals blowing in the wind engulfs the city of Funchal. Most of the plants found only in hothouses in Europe, such as the petunias, begonias and cinerarias grow splendidly out here in the open. The gardens have a superb mix of native plants and foreign additions brought here from all over the world – from Australia, New Zealand, China and Japan, Africa, North and South America, Mexico and Central America and the West Indies. Captain Cook himself planted a tulip tree in the Quinta do Val.

The wonderful mix of indigenous and exotic plants make Funchal's gardens unique. Japanese cherry tree (below).

Quinta do Palheiro Gardens

Set in the hills to the east of Funchal, at an altitude of 500 metres, this is considered by most specialists to be the crowning glory of Madeira's gardens. It was laid out originally in 1801 by the first Conde de Carvalhal, the wealthiest landowner on the island. He first kept the property as a hunting lodge, but then brought over a French landscape gardener to design the formal features which include two avenues of plane trees with a hundred trees on each side, and a one kilometre long row of camellias. His nephew and heir, the second Conde de Carvalhal, was a great *bon vivant*, socializing in the highest European aristocratic circles, and offering the most sumptuous and outrageous parties at Quinta do Palheiro. Legend has it that at one of these parties all the men arrived with a plant from their land of origin, whilst the ladies came dressed with their jewellery, shoes and nothing else.

John Blandy bought the property in 1885 and built an elegant new house designed by the architect of Reid's Hotel, J. S. Clark. It is from this date that the Blandy family have transformed the garden into its magnificent present state. Adam and Christina Blandy live at Palheiro and continue to develop the estate which nowadays includes a golf course, a five star country hotel Casa Velha do Palheiro, and a flower production company.

The gardens are famous for their variety of over ten thousand camellias of every shape colour and size possible. Rare plants from all over the world add enormous interest to the various levels of the garden, including the rare Burmese tree *Sauraja Subspinosa*, the *C. Granthamiana* Camellia from Hong Kong and also uncommon plants from the North Atlantic islands. Beautiful Polonias can be seen flowering in spring together with the enormous Magnolia, and the Telopias and Proteas.

Closest to the house the sunken garden is formally designed with brightly coloured flowers and rockeries. Rolling lawns pass the charming baroque chapel built by the first Count and lead to the *Jardim da Senhora*, a topiary garden with box-edged beds containing sculpted hens, swans, and a moose. For a sharp contrast, pass the Camellia grove and head to the *Ribeiro do Inferno* (brook of hell) where a steamy stream creates a natural hothouse for giant tree ferns and ginger lilies in its deep ravine.

Over 10 000 camellias grow at Palheiro, the Conde de Carvalhal planted a kilometre long avenue of different species in 1801.

Quinta Palmeira

Built in the end of the eighteenth century on the grounds of an ancient chapel dating back to 1580, Quinta Palmeira is set in the Monte parish on an area of land covering around 30 000 square meters. In 1908 Harry Hinton, an important sugar merchant, bought the property at auction and made enormous changes to the gardens, adding the Manueline window frame from a demolished house where Christopher Columbus is said to have stayed. The old palm trees that give the *quinta* its name are magnificently tall as are the Italian cypresses. There are several gardens within the garden, among them the Succulent garden, with plants chosen for their contrasting form or colour, and the Rose Garden which is a traditional English design.

The garden offers a rich choice of indigenous and exotic plants. The rare species include the small tree which is covered in white flowers from December to February *(Pomoea arborescens)* from Honduras and El Salvador, various Dombeya's *(Combretum paniculatum)*, and the Swamp Cypress *(Taxodium distichum)* from the United States. This is the perfect location to observe birds attracted by the tall trees. A wonderful view of Funchal can be seen from below the bougainvillea filled pergolas.

Jardim Botanico da Madeira

The site chosen for the Botanical Garden was the Quinta do Bom Sucesso, which was created in 1960. Formerly it belonged to the Reids family and covers an area of more than 50 000 square meters of gardens. It provides the perfect setting for plants which thrive in permanent spring temperatures. One of the main purposes of the garden is the conservation of indigenous Madeiran plants, especially from its evergreen forest, some of which are very rare and extinct in the wild. Besides the rarities, at least two hundred other native plants can be seen in their natural habitat in the garden. In the drier levels at the higher elevations, there is a very good collection of cacti, one particular group of them transports us to South America. Below, there are tropical and subtropical orchards, and also a woodland garden for orchids. The topiary garden is an excellent place to rest and admire the different sculptures. Lower down and through a different entrance is the Jardim dos Loiros vividly alive with tropical birds, parrots, parakeets and macaws.

Monte Palace Tropical Garden

The garden covers an area of seven hectares of sloping land in the centre of Monte, which originally belonged to the Jesuits in the sixteenth century. The Monte Palace Hotel was created in 1897 amidst majestic lakes and fountains inspired by German palaces. In 1988 the art collector, Joe Berardo, bought Monte Palace and through his foundation set about transforming the gardens into a luxuriant mixture of tropical and indigenous plants. The garden also houses the largest collection of cycads in the world, with every variety possible, mostly from South Africa.

The area reserved for local species from the laurel forest gives a glimpse of how the valley of Funchal looked when the settlers first arrived on the island, and before they set fire to the hills. There are several lakes, and thousand-year-old olive trees have been transplanted here, rescued from the Alentejo when a dam was built there recently.

Jardins do Imperador

Known also as the Quinta Rocha Machado, 'Gordons', and the original Quinta do Monte, this garden has only recently been restored. Built in the first half of the nineteenth century in the Georgian style by David Webster Gordon, it is famous for receiving several distinguished guests such as King Charles and Queen Amelia of Portugal, and the Emperor Karl I of Austria, who died in the yellow room. This is a wonderful example of a Madeiran *quinta*, with a five hundred-year-old chestnut tree watching over the house and spacious lawns in front. There are huge trees in this garden from most corners of the world – including sequoias from North America, cedars from Mexico and Guatemala, callitris from Australia and Tasmania, and some Japanese cedars. There are pine trees from the Mediterranean, magnolias from North America, and camellias from Japan. Among the finest examples of native plants are the Madeira Cheesewood tree which is one of the largest ever seen, dragon trees, and laurels. There is a sunken garden with a marvellous view of the bay of Funchal called the *Jardim Malakof* (created during the Crimean War), which has over sixty flowerbeds lined with box hedging.

Levada Walks

Madeira's water-supply system in open channels is without parallel in the world. Running through vast areas of mountain and countryside, they date as far back as the fifteenth century. Throughout the last five hundred years a continuous battle was fought to bring water to the agricultural plantations, this meant picking around and through mountains, creating at least 40 kilometres of tunnels, and some 2200 kilometres of irrigation channels, all of them built by hand. Sometimes the areas were so difficult to reach that the men were suspended by ropes as they sculpted the hard rock.

The levadas, as they are known, trap the waters high up in the mountains at their source, and carry them along in open channels. They are then released down steep shoots to the land below. The levadas are narrow canals, not wider than a metre and with a depth of around fifty to sixty centimetres. Nearly all the levadas begin from northern or central points on the island, with some of them running for dozens of kilometres and supplying thousands of farmers around the island.

The water is strictly distributed and supervised, by days and minutes per week (the average is about fifteen minutes every fifteen days) to the various villages and plantations, and each levada has a *levadeiro*, or supervisor, to make sure the channels are clean and kept flowing. Even in Funchal several gardens are still fed by the waters that gush down the hills as they once did for the banana plantations.

There are about two hundred levadas in total, most of them state owned, such as the Levada do Rabaçal and the Levada da Serra do Faial, which are the largest ones. Others are in private hands such as the Levada de Santa Luzia in Funchal which was already bringing water to the sugar cane plantations in 1515.

Discovering these levadas is a source of never-ending pleasure, as they offer spectacular walks through accessible country lanes or take one to plunging ravines and frightening tunnels. With an increasing number of people visiting the island specifically to walk these levadas, there has been some attempt to classify them from easy – beginner type walks to the very difficult, long, and sometimes dangerous hikes.

Several guidebooks about the island specialize in levadas and describe in detail how to undertake such walks, with maps and reference points so you can go on your own, or choose the option of joining a guided walking party.

Over 2200 kilometres of levadas have been carved out by hand through and around the mountains of Madeira.

Rabaçal

From hundreds of levadas there are a couple that should not be missed, among them is the greatest of all the Levada do Rabaçal.

Set in the central part of the island, the source of these canals is the Ribeira da Janela, which is the largest river on the island. Major work started in 1835 and they were completed in 1890.

An English lady married to a Portuguese landowner, Isabella de França wrote a journal of her travels in Madeira from 1853–1854. In this she describes the Rabaçal walk leading to twenty-five fountains (Vinte e Cinco Fontes): '*We now began the descent to the Rabaçal, which is by a succession of zigzags, forming what is called a road, cut through a forest of laurel, myrtle, and other evergreens, growing so thickly together, that the whole forest seems one tangled mass of leaves. The descent is perfectly frightful; [...] I thought I had reached the waterfall, and was losing myself in admiration, but we still went on[...]; I looked up, and felt as I can never feel again! There was the glorious waterfall itself, in all its grandeur, and in all its beauty! A tall, tall, semicircular concave rock, covered with a profusion of the most exquisite foliage, of a yet greener green than any of the rest; ferns and mosses, and hanging wreaths, bright scarlet moss cups, white flowering plants, orange coloured fungi [...] all combined to produce a sensation of intense admiration – I should rather call it awe!*'

There are two wonderful levada walks in Rabaçal; one takes thirty minutes each way to the Risco Waterfall, and the other is a more demanding two to three hour walk to twenty-five fountains. The first walk is easily accessible and sometimes crowded, but if you venture past the Risco waterfall a tunnel then takes you beneath the falls, and here it starts getting trickier and slippery but with spectacular views of the ravine. The other route to the twenty-five fountains, leads to a couple of small waterfalls plunging into icy cold pools where some brave visitors jump off the waterfalls and swim in the freezing waters below. For a longer walk follow the Levada Nova do Rabaçal through a tunnel to the other side of the Island, Calheta.

Rabaçal – Risco Vinte e Cinco Fontes – Calheta
3.5 hours
Distance: 10 km
Moderate

Northern Walks

The Pico das Pedras National Park in Santana is the starting point for some of the most superb walks. Among the best is the walk from Pico das Pedras to Queimadas, and then to Caldeirão Verde and Caldeirão do Inferno. The three peaks mountain walk is unlike any other, and is by far the most dramatic as it crosses the highest peaks in Madeira.

Queimadas – Caldeirão Verde – Caldeirão do Inferno – Queimadas

4 hours
Distance: 16 km
Moderate

Queimadas is near Pico das Pedras, and offers a picture of virtually virgin Madeiran forest, with fine examples of laurel, Madeira cedar and picconia. Clearings in this forest reveal fountains, ponds, and carefully tended gardens. If Shakespeare had come to Madeira, the following lines from A Midsummer Night's Dream might well have described Queimadas!

'*Oberon: [...] I know a bank were the wild thyme blows, / Where oxlips and the nodding violet grows, / Quite overcanopied with luscious woodbine, /With sweet musk-roses, and with eglantine. / There sleeps Titania sometime of the night, / Lulled in these flowers with dances and delight; / And there the snake throws her enamelled skin, / Weed wide enough to wrap a fairy in.*' Act II, Scene I.

This is a mild walk that takes about four hours. Ravines and four tunnels lead to the Caldeirão Verde. A thirty minute walk takes you to the Caldeirão do Inferno and some steps climb up to a second levada known as the Levada do Pico Ruivo.

Pico Areeiro – Pico das Torres – Pico Ruivo

3–4 hours
Distance: 14 km
Difficult

A difficult walk, that takes about three to four hours, between Madeira's three highest mountain peaks. Hundreds of steps carved in the rock lead up to Pico das Torres, another steep climb and you reach Pico Ruivo. From the top of Pico Ruivo one can look onto Curral das Freiras, Pico Grande, Paul da Serra and Pico do Areeiro.

Ribeiro Frio – Balcões – Ribeiro Frio

1–2 hours
Distance: 4 km
Moderate

This is an easy walk that gives a delightful taste of what a levada is without too much effort. One of the main attractions here is to explore parts of Madeira's endemic laurel forest *(floresta Laurissilva)* along the Levada do Furado. The scenery of Faial from the Balcões (terraces) viewing point is stunning, and from this spot one can also admire the beautiful valley of Fajã da Nougueira.

Ribeiro Frio – Lamaceiros – Portela

4 hours
Distance: 10 km
Medium difficulty

This is one of the most popular walks on the island. The Levada do Furado passes through Cabeça do Furado onto the Lamaceiros forest post. Portela is the perfect place to catch amazing views of the north coast.

Arts & Crafts

The embroidery of Madeira

THE QUALITY OF the embroidery found on Madeira is second to none, coveted by the major capitals and Royal houses of Europe for the past hundred years . This reputation is based on fine designs and high quality as each piece of embroidery has to undergo several strict inspections before receiving the *gremio* seal from the Madeira Embroidery Guild.

The delicate embroidery done at Bordal (above and previous page). The Bernard Shaw suite at Reid's has vintage embroidery bedspreads.

One of the most important influences on the industry was the daughter of a local English shipper, Miss Phelps, who came to Madeira in the 1850's. Quickly noticing how good the local women were with their hands, she introduced them to the technique of broderie anglaise, which they were very eager to learn. Miss Phelps sent some of the more intricate pieces to England. These were followed by several orders placed and the establishing of a new industry. In just thirty years the style became known as broderie Madere. The embroidery industry soon gave thousands of families a new income, and by 1906 there were thirty thousand rural and two thousand professional embroiderers in Funchal. Most of the work was done at home, with the design and finishing touches made in the Funchal factories.

The Germans transformed this cottage industry into a worldwide trade, introducing faster methods and increasing production. During the First World War the Germans living in Madeira were interned and their businesses confiscated. This saw a rise in foreign firms entering the market to take the place of the lucrative German firms. The Americans of Syrian origin dominated the trade for a while, and they soon flooded the world market with inferior quality pillowcases. The effect on Madeira's reputation was immediate and trade slumped from 1916–1925.

Imperial Linens was formed in 1925 by two American entrepreneurs, Charlie Rolland and Leo Behrens who set about changing the embroidery style, introducing new techniques brought from abroad. In so doing they created the Madeira embroidery as we know it. New motifs were created using Madeira's flowers as inspiration, also adding shells, plumes and daily scenes from Funchal life. One of the best known works of the Imperial Linens Company was the Princess Grace tablecloth, designed at the time of her wedding to Prince Rainier of Monaco, by a gifted German designer, Herman Klein.

From the initial idea to the finished embroidery piece there are several stages. First of all the design is created, then the high quality fabrics, colours and threads are chosen and imported. Stitches are decided upon and counted, the design is drawn on a paper and sent to the *picotagem* – perforating department. The design leaves the factory for the countryside, were an agent delivers it to the embroiderers. The skill of these women is legendary; they sit in groups with as many as three generation working side-by-side, embroidering rapidly and teaching the younger ones their craft.

After returning the embroidery to the factories it has to pass several checks before finally receiving the *Gremio* seal and the authentication tag.

Tapestry

There are records of tapestry works dating back to the eighteenth century, however it was only when the German artist Herbert Kiekeben came to Madeira in 1938 that a cottage industry was born. He painted his still-lives and copies of old masters onto a canvas and this was then sown into a tapestry. Most of the tapestries sold in Madeira are replicas of old masters and don't strive for great originality. Among the artefacts produced are carpets, chair covers, handbags and pillows.

Musical instruments

Music is another renowned Madeiran art form. The Madeirans are cheerful and always up for a party. This can be seen in the jolly rhythm of their music and songs. Among the unique musical instruments are the *braguinha*, a very small four-stringed guitar that was brought with the first settlers; this was taken to Hawaii in the nineteenth century by a Madeiran emigrant who set up shop selling them. They were re-baptised as ukuleles (jumping fleas). The *rajão* and *viola de arme* are also string instruments, and the *brinquinho* which keeps step to the sound of the folklore songs, consists of colourful circles with dolls dressed in typical costumes up a stick, which clap each time there are tugged. Banda d'Alem and Xarabanda are the two local bands that ensure that Madeira's music is passed on to new generations – carrying out extensive field work, collecting traditional lyrics and music from around the Island. Banda d'Alem has around six musicians that sing and play traditional instruments, updating the beats to a younger audience.

The brinquinho, a musical toy, comes to life as it keeps step to the folk dances.

Wickers

The wicker industry started in Camacha on the south-eastern part of the island, around 1850, when many British families had their summerhouses out there. Willian Hinton brought examples back from Italy that could be copied by the local craftsmen, and soon they were producing cane furniture for Germany, Britain and the Funchal hotels. Cone-shaped wicker baskets for carrying grapes had existed on the island for centuries, known as *barraleiros*, but it was only in the nineteenth century that the more sophisticated wicker furniture was made.

Willows are grown in damp valleys near streams – in places such as Camacha, Santo da Serra, S. Vicente, and S. Jorge. The shoots are trimmed near the ground in the first months of the year, placed in water and left until they start to sprout. They are then peeled and dried, ready to use. Among the artefacts produced are cane chairs, tables, baskets, hampers, animal sculptures, shelves and much more. Most of these items are exported to the United States, South Africa, Canada and Italy.

Camacha is still the centre of this small industry, where skilful artisans can be seen weaving in the basement of the Café Relógio.

Generations of families have learnt the craft of wicker making at Camacha.

BUAL
1908
OSSART GORDON
MADEIRA

Wine & Food

29
000
VAZIA
A

OVER THE CENTURIES, Madeira has gained a reputation for its famous wine, and ultimately become synonymous with it. This unique wine is unparalleled in the world, with a sweet fresh intensity that gets better with the passing years. Wines over a hundred years hold notably well and Madeira has the oldest vintages.

Madeira wine was catapulted onto the world stage in the seventeenth century, and it became the favourite wine of the American colonies. George Washington got through a pint a night, and a glass of Madeira sealed the signing of the American Declaration of Independence. Russia was addicted as it was a favourite at the Tsar's court and it was even used for bait to poison Rasputin. In the nineteenth and early twentieth century such French authors as Honoré Balzac, the Marquis de Sade and Alexandre Dumas praised Madeira wine.

The wine's distinctive taste is the result of an accident that happened in the 1700's. One unsold shipment travelled around the world as ballast – twice crossing the equator and back to the island, undergoing temperatures as high as 45º, and then cooling for six months. It was found to be absolutely delicious and astonishingly mature. Nowadays Madeira is subjected to the same intense heat but it doesn't have to travel so far for the sublime taste. *Estufas* are ovens that produce tropical heat for cheaper wines, whereas finer wines are heated gently in warm rooms for four or five months. At around the same time brandy was added to fortify the Madeira wine which halted the fermentation and made the wine sweeter.

Madeira wine has the oldest vintages in the world.

'Why this same Madeira-wine has made me as light as a grasshopper'

WILLIAM CONGREVE, *The Old Bachelor* (1693)

Where are the vineyards?
All over the island.

In the nineteenth century Madeira wine very nearly disappeared as it was struck by the double disaster of *Oidium Tucker* (mildew) and the fungus *Phylloxera Vastatrix*. This caused huge poverty and a flow of emigration to Brazil. Fifty-five of the seventy British wine merchants closed their businesses and left Madeira. As a result, the classical vines were replaced by the American hybrid varieties which were more resistant to the diseases. During the First World War stocks of good Madeira were used, and led to a rise in the wine's value and popularity. Madeira's fortunes have begun to rise again, after a depressing period when it was only used for cooking. The wine producers on the island are striving to re-capture their world market, with greater quality control, re-planting the classical vines, and creating exciting new blends.

Madeira's vineyards are scattered throughout the coast of the island, and there are about fourteen thousand plots of ground growing vines. Most of the old vineyards are still found on walled terraces constructed centuries ago on quite small pieces of land.

The varieties used to produce fortified wine make up just over 50 % of all grapes grown on the island; the rest are used to make table wine. The grapes for producing fortified Madeira wine all come from the *Vitis vinifera* genus which are used in the four classical types of Madeira.

In September the countryside is full of grape pickers, and important wine festivals are celebrated from Câmara de Lobos to Santana. The grapes are picked from mid-August to early November, and most are taken whole to the lodges where they are then pressed. Since joining the EU, substantial investment has improved the techniques and practices of the local wine industry. Once the grapes are received at the winery they are poured in hoppers, fortified, and then rested. Tinta Negra Mole undergoes a process of *estufagem*, which is illegal for the vintage wines that have to mature naturally in casks, preferably American oak. An oenologist will then monitor the progress of the vintage wines year by year.

'If I had a thousand sons, the first humane principle I would teach them should be – to forswear thin potations, and to addict themselves to sack'

WILLIAM SHAKESPEARE, *King Henry IV, part I, IV. III*

Madeira wine is characterized by its distinctive taste of caramelized sugar that comes from wood-ageing. The best glass to taste this wine is the tulip-shaped medium glass which releases the bouquet. The four main types of Madeira wines are named after their vines: Malvasia (Malmsey), Boal (Bual), Verdelho, Sercial.

Malvazia Has a light tawny colour. It is the sweetest and most popular kind. Tasting of vanilla toffee with hints of marmalade, it is perfect for an after dinner digestive.

Boal Is a tortoiseshell colour, the darkest shade of all varieties. With a bouquet of caramel and dried fruit, this smoky lighter wine is excellent as a dessert wine.

Verdelho Is golden coloured and even drier than Boal. Slightly honeyed with hints of citrus fruits, it can be sipped as an aperitif, with soup or again after dinner.

Sercial Is the driest variety and has the palest colour. The taste is reminiscent of dried fruits and oranges and is described as an ideal aperitif wine to accompany hors d'oeuvres.

The other varieties of Madeira include: Tinta Negra Mole, Bastardo, Terrantez and Moscatel.

Tinta Negra Mole Is mass produced and the most adaptable wine, changing quality to acquire the characteristics of the four main grapes depending on which altitude or treatment it receives from the wine-makers. Tinta Negra Mole grape provides over 90 % of the grapes used in Madeira wine. It cannot be sold legally under its own name although the wine it produces is superb.

Bastardo Is a rarity from the past, the grapes are sweet but the wine is mostly made in a dry style. It is produced with the same grape used to make Port.

Terrantez First recorded in Madeira in the eighteenth century, it comes from a very rare white grape variety, which produces a highly scented and sweet Madeira.

Moscatel Is very scarce on the island and mostly used for blending purposes, as it is quite expensive due to its popularity as a table wine. The grapes are large and pale green with a sweet flavour.

Other classifications for Madeira wine include: Rainwater, Vintage and Solera.

Rainwater Madeira A blend of Verdelho and Tinta Negra Mole, the wine gets its name from a consignment of Madeira bound for Boston in the eighteenth century that was accidentally diluted by rain. This less deeply flavoured wine has been a huge hit with the American market ever since.

Vintage Madeira Madeira has an incredibly old vintage, the oldest in the world, and there are still pre-phylloxera bottles around. Currently for a wine to be considered a vintage it must be at least twenty years in cask, and then stand in the bottle for two years before going on sale. The oldest vintage dates from 1715.

Solera Madeira Authentic soleras are delicious and can produce the best wines. This can be a mixture of vintages or an established vintage with a good young wine. The date on the bottle simply indicates the vintage of the wine with which the solera was started. No more Soleras are being made as very strict regulations have disallowed unbottled stocks from coming onto the market.

Food in the region

The sea is Madeira's natural extension, and the local fishermen are masters at taking the best advantage of it. Freshly caught fish arrives every day and can be seen at the lively coastal markets.

The best fish specialities on the island are the fresh tuna, fried horse mackerel known as *chicharros,* and of course the scabbard fish accompanied with passion fruit or banana. Limpets are a local favourite made with a hint of butter and sprinkled with lemon, and scabbard fish eggs are superb in a vinaigrette sauce.

Simple recipes with excellent ingredients are the secret to Madeira's cuisine. The official delicacy is called *espetada,* which consists of beef cubes skewered on a laurel stick and then barbecued over an open fire. This speciality is accompanied by fried maize and *bolo do caco.* This is a round, flat bread made of wheat flour and traditionally cooked on a piece of roof tile on the grill. The other great speciality is *carne vinha d'alhos,* normally eaten on Christmas day, prepared with pork.

The Madeira countryside is dotted with fruit-bearing trees, and every scrap of land is cultivated. These terraced patches produce especially delicious fruits which are transformed into heavenly puddings or sorbets. The local queijada, a sweet pastry made with cheese is mouthwatering – and the famous *bolo de mel,* a rich spicy molasses cake, is the perfect accompaniment to Madeira wine.

In Porto Santo the choice of food is not overwhelming, however what does exist is simply delicious. The local lobster – *cavaco* is superb but very hard to come by. Excellent specialities include various octopus dishes, barbecued chicken, and beef *espetada.* The grapes, watermelons and melons all have a delicately sweet flavour.

Scabbard fish laid out in rows in Funchal market.

Terrine of Foie Gras Marinated with Malmsey Madeira Wine
Serves 6

The Terrine
Clean the fresh *foie gras* by removing the veins and any sinew. Then place it in the base of a stainless steel tray and spread it out to the edges. Pour in the mixed marinade and distribute evenly over the *foie gras*. Marinade over night in the fridge. Remove from the fridge and slice into even strips to the same dimension as your terrine. Then place the strips of marinated *foie gras* on top of each other within the terrine. Using a flat object of similar dimension to your terrine (the base of another terrine) press down on the terrine of *foie gras* to remove any air. Place the marinated *foie gras* into the oven for 35 minutes at 75°C. After removing the terrine from the oven allow to cool for about 1 hour and then place in the fridge for at least 24 hours (48 hours is ideal). Should you wish to remove the excess fat, place the same weighted object on top of the terrine while still warm to force the liquid fat up the sides of the terrine. Allow to cool and then trim the fat once solidified. By retaining the fat as a seal, your terrine may be refrigerated up to 7 days as opposed to 3 – 4 days.

For the sauce
Reduce the vinegar and honey together with the chopped eucalyptus leaf to about 75%. Add the stock and simmer gently for 15 minutes. Pass the resulting mixture through a fine strainer. Warm gently before serving.

The Accompaniment
Place a few fine slices of smoked duck against the sliced terrine. Drizzle the mesclun salad with walnut oil. Serve with toasted brioche

Terrine of Foie Gras Marinated with Malmsey Madeira Wine

Wine notes
Blandy's Malmsey Madeira Wine – The older the better

Recipe by BENOIT SINTHÔN,
courtesy of Estalagem Casa Velha do Palheiro

Ingredients
500 g foie gras frais

Marinade
6 g Salt
1.5 g Pepper
1 g Sugar
12.5 ml Malmsey Madeira wine

Eucalyptus & Honey Sauce
50 ml Vinegar
100 ml Honey
1 Roughly chopped eucalyptus leaf
200 ml Duck stock (or beef if not available)

Accompaniment
75 g Sliced smoked duck breast
250 g Mesclun salad (mixed salad)
Brioche

Cipriani Salad

Serves 4

Lobsters

Place all the ingredients mentioned above with the exception of the lobsters, in boiling water and leave for five minutes. Then add the two lobsters and let cook for fifteen -sixteen minutes. Remove from water and let cool.

Making the Salad

Slice the avocados and mushrooms in small cubes. Add the tomato, ½ dl of balsamic vinegar, ½ dl of olive oil, chopped coriander, the salt and pepper to taste and mix it all together. With the remaining balsamic vinegar and olive oil make a vinaigrette sauce. Decorate the plate with green salad and radicchio leaves. At the centre of the plate place the avocado and mushroom salad. Then around the salad place the slices of the lobster. The coriander leaves are placed on top of the salad as decoration. Use the paprika for colour and season the plate with the prepared vinaigrette.

Wine Notes

Quinta do Cidrô Chardonnay, Douro, Portugal, White

MARIO CALLIGARI, Executive Chef, Vila Cipriani

Lobster Ingredients

2 Lobsters 500 g each
1 Carrot
1 Onion
1 Laurel leaf
10 g Black grain pepper
10 g Celery
1 dl Vinegar
5 l Water
Salt to taste

Salad Ingredients

2 Avocado pears 200g each
4 Radicchio salad leaves
4 Green salad leaves
10 g Chopped coriander and some leaves to decorate
1½ dl Fresh sliced tomato
1 dl Balsamic vinegar
2 dl Olive oil
100 g Cultivated mushrooms
10 g Paprika
Salt, pepper to taste

Bife de Atum
á Joe's Bilhar
Serves 4

The secret to this recipe is that all the tuna served in Joe's Bar is caught by the owners off the coast of Madeira, José Antonio and Roberto Ribeiro are both expert big game fishermen and as soon as they catch a tuna it is immediately killed and bled – which makes the flesh white and tender, unlike the commercial tuna which struggles for hours and ends up with tough dark red meat.

Sprinkle the tuna steaks with sea salt and grill on a hot plate. Once grilled pour over the sauce. Serve with fried maize or boiled potatoes and salad.

For the sauce
Place the olive oil, garlic, oregano and white wine in a pan. Let it boil and simmer for two minutes, and put salt according to taste.

Joe's Tuna Steak

Ingredients
600 g Tuna fillet steaks
Sea Salt

Sauce
Olive oil
Garlic
Oregano
White wine
Sea salt

Wine Notes
Winter – Foral, Grande Escolha, 2001, Douro, Portugal, Red
Summer – Duas Quintas, 2002, Douro, Portugal, White

Recipe courtesy of José ANTONIO RIBEIRO,
Joe's Bar – Quinta da Penha de França

Risotto de Lapas e Espada

Serves 4

Cut the scabbard fillets in four pieces, then roll around a rounded shape and tie with the leek leaves. Steam until tender. Separately boil the fish stock and water for three minutes. Then fry the onions with garlic and olive oil in a pan, add the limpets, the rice and remains of fish stock and cook for ten minutes. When the rice is soft add the tomato, butter, parmesan cheese and parsley. Place the fish in a deep dish, pour the limpet risotto inside the scabbard ring.

For the sauce

Melt the remaining butter and pour around the scabbard.

Scabbard Fish and Limpet Risotto

Wine notes

Casa de Pancas, Chardonnay & Arinto, 2003, Estremadura, Portugal, White

ALCINO MARQUES,

Executive Chef, Vila Porto Mare

Porto Bay Hotels & Resorts

Chef Alcino at the Vila Porto Mare likes to give a modern twist to traditional Madeiran ingredients.

Ingredients

600 g Scabbard fish fillets

200 g Risotto

200 g Limpets (shelled)

150 g Tomato cubes

100 g Onion, diced

70 cl. Olive oil

1l. Fish stock

10 g Salt

5 g Pepper

10 g Parsley, chopped

50 g Leek leaves

10 g Garlic, chopped

100 g Butter

20 g Parmesan cheese

Espetada de Vaca Regional e Milho Frito

Serves 4

Cut the meat into cubes with about 25–30g each, place on the laurel skewers and season with salt, garlic, pepper and laurel. Grill on barbecue.

For the maize, place the onions and olive oil in a pan and cook, add water and lard and next add the corn flour – mixing well with a stick until it starts to boil. Let it cook for about one hour, mixing constantly, then add the diced cabbage, salt and let boil for a couple of minutes. Place on a tray and let cool, and then cut into triangles or any other shape you want. Finally heat some oil in a frying pan and fry the maize until it is crispy.
Make a butter sauce with garlic and chopped parsley.

Beef Espetada and Fried Maize

Wine Notes
Vertente, Dirk Niepoort & Jorge Serôdio Borges, 2001, Douro, Portugal, Red

FELIPE ALVES,
Executive Chef, Hotel Porto Santa Maria,
Porto Bay Hotels & Resorts

Ingredients

680 g Beef loin with a bit of fat
100 g Butter
15 g Parsley, chopped
20 g Garlic, diced
20 g Coarse Salt
5 g Pepper
4 Laurel twigs for skewers
5 g Bay leaves

For the fried maize

500 g White corn flour
50 g Cabbage, diced
15 g Pork lard
25 g Onion, diced
5 cl Olive oil
3 cl Water
10 g Salt
Oil for frying

Filete de Porco em Vinha d'Alhos

Serves 4

Marinate the pork fillets with the wine, vinegar, garlic, paprika, pepper, salt and summer savoy, and leave all ingredients overnight to absorb flavours. Cook all the ingredients in a casserole with the marinade included at a low fire for about one hour until the meat is soft and tender. Cut the two *bolo do caco* breads (flat round shaped country bread) in halves, soak each half in the marinade and pan fry until it gets golden brown. Boil the burnet in salted water. Sauté the boiled burnet with olive oil, parsley and pepper. Pan fry the potatoes with parsley, salt and pepper.

For the sauce

Reduce the marinade, pass the resulting mixture through a fine strainer and then over the meat.

Pork Fillet in Vinegar and Garlic Marinade

Wine Notes

Herdade Porto da Bouga, António Saramago, 2001, Alentejo, Portugal, Red

ALCINO MARQUES,
Executive Chef, Vila Porto Mare,
Porto Bay Hotels & Resorts

Ingredients

640 g Pork fillets
1l. White wine (good quality)
50 cl. Wine vinegar
30 g Garlic crushed with skin
15 g Summer savoy
10 g Paprika
5 g Pepper
30 g Coarse Salt
2 Bolo do caco breads
150 g Burnet in cubes
150 g Potatoes in cubes
15 g Parsley
1l. Olive oil
5 g Bay leaf

Ingredients
5 cl Milk
190 g Banana puree
80 g Sugar
30 g Corn starch
200 g Egg whites
10 g Icing sugar

Sauce
100 g Summer Fruits (blackberries, raspberries, blueberries)
5 cl. Water
1 Lemon, juice
35 g Sugar
10 g Glucose

Soufflé Quente de Banana com Molho de Frutos Silvestres
Serves 4

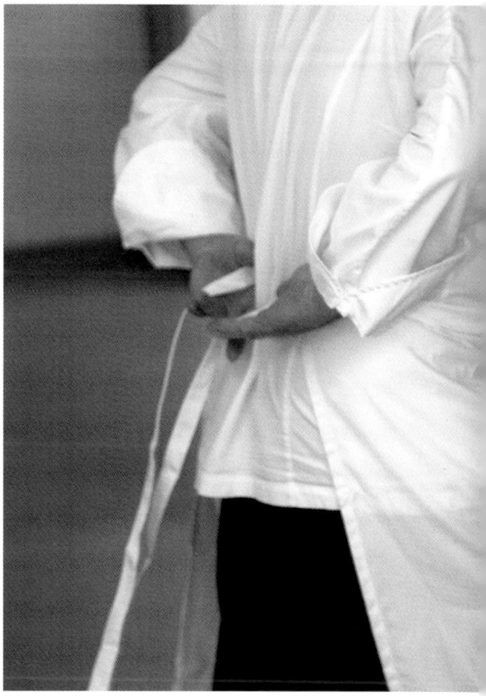

Heat the milk, sugar and banana puree (made with fresh bananas) in a pan, and add the flour (diluted with cold water), bring to boil. When cool fold in the whisked egg whites. Line the moulds with butter and sprinkled sugar; then pour the mixture into the soufflé moulds until they are half full.
Cook in the oven at a medium temperature of around 190°C for fifteen minutes, until the soufflé has risen and is looking golden.

For the sauce
Place the berries and sugar in a pan, add the lemon juice, water and glucose. Bring to boil for several minutes until the juice thickens. Serve the sauce separately at the table. With a spoon pierce a hole in the centre of the soufflé and pour in the warm sauce. Serve immediately after leaving the oven and dust with icing sugar.

Banana Soufflé with Wild Berries Coulis

Wine Notes
Blandy's Malmsey, 1978, Madeira, Portugal

José Luis Silva,
Pastry Chef, Vila Porto Mare,
Porto Bay Hotels & Resorts

Cheesecake de Maracujá

Serves 4

For the base

Process the biscuits until they are like small crumbs. Then add the margarine and icing sugar, pulse the ingredients together. Flatten the dough, cutting circular shapes to use as the base of each pudding, putting them in the fridge to set while making the topping.

For the filling

Place the gelatine in cold water. In a separate dish beat the cream gently and then add the condensed milk. Add the mashed curd cheese and mixing everything together thoroughly. Join the passion fruit pulp and lemon juice until it is well mixed. Melt the gelatine and pour it slowly onto the passion fruit mixture until it is all blended.
The raspberry pulp is poured over and around the cheesecake and the perfect accompaniment is a scoop of passion fruit ice cream.

Passion Fruit Cheesecake

Ingredients

120 g Digestive biscuits
60 g Margarine
60 g Icing sugar
100 g Cream
24 g Condensed milk
80 g Curd Cheese
2 un. Gelatine sheets
4 un. Passion fruit pulp
1 un. Lemon, juice

40 g Raspberry pulp
4 un. Passion fruit ice cream scoops

Wine Notes

Ferreira Duque Bragança 20 y.o., J.M.S. Franco, Portugal, Red port

BENOIT SINTHÔN, Executive Chef, The Cliff Bay, Porto Bay Hotels & Resorts

The executive chef of the Cliff Bay, Benoit Sinthôn, rises early to visit the Funchal market, were he personally chooses the best fish and fruits.

Porto Santo, Desertas & Selvagens

RISING MAJESTICALLY FROM the Atlantic Ocean, the island of Porto Santo lies seventy-five kilometres northeast of Funchal, a fifteen minute plane ride or two hour boat journey away. It is the second largest island of the Madeiran archipelago, and the only other inhabited one (with around five thousand estimated residents), and an area of forty one square meters, measuring eleven kilometres long and six kilometres wide. The bareness of its landscape and yellow sandy beach is in stark contrast with the green valleys of Madeira. Here time stops, cares disappear and the only pressing worry is when the ice-cream stand will open next. The Gulf Stream offers constantly hot temperatures, as it does in Madeira – and the long beach is the ideal place to enjoy this warmth.

Porto Santo is also of volcanic origin – although all volcanic activity is extinct now. It is much older than Madeira, dating from the Miocene period (13,5 million years old), and is flat except for the two peaks that stand at each extremity of the island. The highest points on the island are Pico do Facho (517 metres) and Pico do Castelo (438 metres). Apart from the main island there are also various tiny islets, which are excellent diving points – the largest being Ilheu de Baixo or Cal, and Ilheu de Cima.

The idyllic 9-kilometre beach of Porto Santo stretches out way into the horizon.

Among the various things that make Porto Santo unique are the sea, beach, and grapes.

The sea is very inviting, with completely unpolluted transparent turquoise blue waters, and waves that break gently on the shore. The beach doesn't need a lifeguard, as there are no currents to drag one out or depressions to fall into – just flat shallow sand, and kilometres of an idyllic, spacious beach.

The beach is a straight runway of pale yellow sand nine kilometres long. Here one can walk endlessly, sometimes without passing a single person, except during July or August when the neighbouring Madeirans come for their holidays. The sand here is known for its therapeutic qualities, and occasionally someone can be seen buried with only their head popping out.

One of the few reasons for leaving the beach is to fetch some grapes. These are sold by the side of the road, pale green in appearance, with a sweet watery taste – the cooling effect is immediate. Grapes are grown on the arid agricultural patches, and the sandy earth and sea air gives them their particular Porto Santo taste. These grapes also produce a distinctive Madeira wine and have rare grape varieties still growing here such as *Barrete de Frade* and *Tinta Molar*, which are extinct in Madeira.

The absence of rocks, seaweed or currents make this, without doubt, one of the best beaches in the world.

Porto Santo Island was the very first of the Portuguese overseas discoveries, stumbled onto by accident in 1419 by a small ship of explorers serving Prince Henry the Navigator, who were caught in a storm off the coast of Africa. Just as they had lost all hope of ever seeing land, their ship came across Porto Santo (Sacred Port). The island was given to Bartolomeu Perestrelo, an Italian seaman working for Prince Henry, who became the first Donatory Captain, and his descendants went on to rule in an unbroken line until the Spanish occupation in 1580.

Filipa Moniz, the daughter of Bartolomeu Perestrelo, married Christopher Columbus in 1478, and they had a son, Diogo. She died shortly after the birth of their son, and Columbus left the island. The house where they may have lived together in Porto Santo is now a museum dedicated to the Genovese explorer, and texts found on the island of Porto Santo in 1848 and 1862 state that Christopher Columbus inherited his father-in-law's manuscripts, and with them discovered the New World.

Colonizing Porto Santo proved to be a very tough job, and although it seems to have developed rapidly in the first hundred and fifty years of its occupation it then stagnated due to a series of difficulties. Among the greatest problems facing the settlers were a naturally barren soil (made worse by the residents chopping down all existing trees to use in construction), neglect by the local and central government, plagues, and relentless attacks by pirates.

From the fifteenth to the eighteenth century Porto Santo was in a state of constant siege, with the population having to flee to the hills to escape the savage onslaughts that came with each visit by Algerian, Moorish, French, and English pirates. These hardships, which caused real misery and famine, drove most of the population to leave the island, emigrating to Madeira or Brazil.

If not for the draconian laws imposed in 1770 by the Marques de Pombal, prime minister under King D. José, the island would soon have been totally uninhabited. Most of the landowners on Porto Santo lived in Madeira or the continent, and their colons worked the land, handing over half of their production, and living in abject poverty. Legislation was passed to protect the colons and those who worked the land, making life at least bearable.

During the nineteenth century Porto Santo had a mining venture, extracting limestone from Ilheu de Baixo (which is why it became known as Ilheu do Cal).

Later, a serious drought in the 1940's, which lasted eight years, finally led to some investment from the Portuguese Salazar government. A plan was hatched to develop agriculture and reforest certain parts of the island. In 1954 a new irrigation dam was finished, electricity was brought to Vila Baleira, the capital of Porto Santo, and drinking water was supplied to the urban population.

Porto Santo has recently been the focus of a major development scheme by the Sociedade de Desenvolvimento do Porto Santo (set up by the local Madeira government) which counts among many other projects a fabulous new golf course designed by Seve Ballesteros that will eventually have forty five holes, a new tennis club, beach games area, a renovated riding centre, and a series of bars in the place known as *Penedo do Sono* overlooking the marina, that jazz up the Porto Santo nightlife.

The colours of Porto Santo are bright and drenched in sunshine, and every blue imaginable can be found on this tiny island.

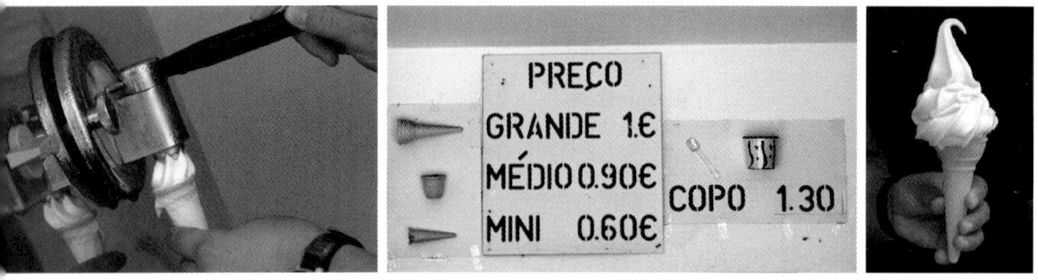

The famous lambeca ice creams have been in Vila Baleira for over four decades

Exploring Porto Santo

Most people first reach the island on the luxurious new ferry *Lobo Marinho* (Sea Wolf) that makes the crossing between Madeira and Porto Santo. The ferry makes the journey in absolute comfort in just over two hours, with a cinema, various sunbathing decks, restaurants and entertainment areas to while away the crossing in style. The *Lobo Marinho* takes passengers and cars, making it the ideal vehicle for getting to Porto Santo, even if only for a day trip. The Porto Santo marina is surrounded by hills and here cruises, yachts and fishing boats all lay anchor.

Vila Baleira, founded by Bartolomeu Perestrelo, remains the only major town and is a charmingly relaxing place with hardly any traffic, and where most of the people gather around the Largo do Pelourinho in the cafés or on the benches. The former town hall dates to the sixteenth century, and even though the Igreja da Nossa Senhora da Piedade was torched several times by pirates a few original Gothic features can still be seen in the church.

Just behind the church the Christopher Columbus museum has original examples of cereal storage pits, and memorabilia of the famous explorer. Back in the main square is a favourite Porto Santo institution – the *lambecas* (little licks) ice cream stand, which still uses the same machine it did forty-three years ago when it opened on the same spot. The ice creams are very refreshing, made special by the Porto Santo water and mysterious ingredients the flavours change from hour to hour, so one keeps coming back throughout the day.

The colourful new fish market is just in front of the beach, and is the best place to see some barracuda, tuna or other fish the locals have brought in. The fishermen in Porto Santo are extremely gifted, and seem to known instinctively where to drop the line. Most of their catch never reaches the supermarket, but goes directly to the restaurants or family. The traditional Porto Santo straw hats can be bought from the arts & crafts centre or from the women who make them in the Serra de Fora area. These light hats have an attractive sand colour, and fend off the hot sun.

Driving down the main road by the sea towards the westernmost point of the island, is Pico das Flores at 184 metres, which has a good view of Madeira and the Desertas. This part of the island is quite exposed and the sun scorches mercilessly, thankfully the Calheta beach down bellow offers instant refreshment with its transparent blue waters looking onto the nearby islet Ilheu de Baixo. Taking a private boat along the coast, there are several sheltered bays to explore and have a private swim. It is also fun to gather limpets, the small sea animals with a shell that hold on tightly to the rocks, in the area around Ilheu de Baixo.

Back along the road there are several places to occupy your time. First up is the riding centre, which keeps several horses so one can explore the central part of Porto Santo through mountain tracks and back paths – this is always a good alternative if the weather is acting up. Further down the road is the thalassotherapy centre, which is the ideal place to relax, have a massage, and try the local therapeutic treatments that use sand and water. Also on the western part of the island stands the new Porto Santo golf club lying at the feet of Pico Ana Ferreira, just past the tennis club. From here the panoramic picture is something to be seen. Several holes are played just near the sea or over it, with the north coast acting as the perfect backdrop to a unique course.

To the north of Vila Baleira is Pico do Castelo, where those who live in Vila Baleira escaped from the pirates. It is slowly being reforested. At Pico do Castelo bonfires were lit in the past to warn Machico village in Madeira Island of the approaching pirates.

Down by the sea on the north coast, the place known as Fonte da Areia has intriguing sand patterns sculpted by the wind and water.

The islets around Porto Santo can be visited by boat, on Ilheu do Ferro there is a little quay for landing and it has rabbits, seabirds, spiders and a small unguarded lighthouse at the top. The lighthouse on Ilheu de Cima dates from 1900.

With droughts and pirates long gone, the focus now is on fun and making the most of the islands natural attractions.

Vines grow on the sand, trained on the ground without support right up to the beach.

When Porto Santo was colonized in the fifteenth century it was covered in trees and shrubs, mostly consisting of cedars, laurels, olive and dragon trees. The colons unwittingly started a process that would leave the landscape desert-like, with sand constantly gaining ground on the few bits of cultivated land, and the resulting landscape is a dry type of grassland quite Mediterranean in appearance. Nowadays the vegetation on the island is essentially made up of small-scale plantations of exotic conifers, and a few introduced species such as the small tamarisk tree *(Tamaric gallica)*.

The dragon trees were tapped for their *dragon blood*, a highly sought after resin used for red dyes and paints. The indigenous plants still found on the island include the ironwood bush, heather, and the Madeira shrubby bittersweet bush. Several plants were subsequently introduced on the island such as the palm trees, pine trees, jacarandas and the silver poplar tree.

When Porto Santo was discovered, lizards and birds were the largest animals on the island. Bartolomeu Perestrelo imported rabbits in the 1420's. They soon multiplied and became a terrible nuisance, eating all the crops and leaving the landscape completely bare. There are also at least forty-four snails peculiar to Porto Santo.

The waters surrounding Porto Santo are full of spotted dolphins, sperm whales, turtles, and all kinds of fish. Along the coast various types of molluscs are found – limpets, periwinkles, small crabs, and rarely *cavaco* lobsters.

Simplicity reigns; the traditional architecture is a fusion of Portuguese and Moorish influences.

Fish of every shape and size make their way to the market.

Atum Posta
Bicuda
Pargo
Gata

What better way to watch the sun set than in Calheta beach savouring a delicious cavaco with white wine?

The food in Porto Santo is refreshingly simple with many dishes similar to those found in Madeira. Among the most sought after is the octopus, prepared in a rich sauce made of tomato, onion and spices. Barbecued chicken and meat *espetada* are also favourites. Right on the beach there are several bars and restaurants, all serving limpets, shrimp, octopus and small meat cubes in a tomato sauce called *picadinho.*

The local wine can't be bought in the supermarket and doesn't even have its own label. The vines were planted here before those in Madeira – most of the vineyards nowadays border the airport runway (which took up the best cultivation land, and led to a declining production in grapes), and can also be seen in small plots in Camacha and on the dunes by the beach. The vines grow on sand, making them resistant to *Phylloxera*, and are trained over the ground without supports. Listrão, the table grape is widely cultivated here to make house wine, bottles can be bought in the little stalls by the side of the road or in the wine lodges near Pico da Ana Ferreira.

Nightfall is just the beginning, with bars and beach parties livening up the evenings.

The Desertas

The three islands that form the Desertas, Deserta Grande, Ilhéu Chão, and Bugio are now an important bird and marine life sanctuary, protecting the very rare seal, *Monachus monachus*. Lying just 30 kilometres southeast of Madeira, the reserve covers all three islands, a total area of 9672 hectares. They are joined underwater to the Ponta de São Lourenço (the easternmost point of Madeira) at a depth of one hundred and fifty metres. The dominant reddish and orange brown colourings that distinguish the islands are explained by their volcanic origin.

These islands were never colonized due to the lack of drinking water and difficult terrain, although some attempts were made early on. Records show that in the sixteenth century wheat was grown on Deserta Grande to feed the cattle that had been introduced. Fragments of history about the islands have survived. Back in 1564, for example, a group of shepherds on Deserta Grande confronted some eighty English pirates, hurling rocks at them as they tried to escape down the cliffs. Later, during the Second World War, the island served as a lookout for German submarines.

Over the years the islands belonged to different Madeiran families, and in 1971 the Portuguese state bought them from the Rocha Machado family.

What little vegetation exists on these islands is essentially herbaceous, as the animals introduced here ate their way through most of the landscape, changing the natural flora and accelerating erosion.

Apart from the colony of twenty or so protected seals, the preserve is also an important haven for sea birds, some of them are very rare, such as the Freira do Bugio *(Peterodroma feae)*, which is found only on the Ilheu do Bugio and in the Cape Verde islands off the coast of Africa.

The Deserta Grande is home to a deadly tarantula *(Lycosa ingens)*, and although vegetation is very sparse, made worse over time by rabbits, rats, and goats, there are more than two hundred plant species on the islands.

The Selvagens or Savage Islands

Lying almost three hundred kilometres south of Funchal, the Selvagens are closer to the Canary Islands than to Madeira, but were officially discovered by a Portuguese explorer, Diogo Gomes, in the fifteenth century. Today they act as a vital sanctuary for wildlife made up mainly of nesting sea birds. The islands cannot be visited without special permission. The Selvagem Grande is flat with one hundred metre cliffs plunging into the sea, dating twenty eight million years since its formation. The climate is maritime subtropical, with the northeast winds bringing high temperatures and sand from the Sahara desert. Selvagem Pequena and Ilheu de Fora are both relics of underwater volcano peaks and are now mostly covered in limestone sand.

The lack of any source of drinking water defeated all attempts at colonizing these inhospitable islands though a few ruined walls can still be found on the Selvagem Grande. Goats and rabbits were introduced here in the fifteenth century, and nearly ate the island bare. For centuries, however, Selvagem Grande provided a steady income to their owners from the export of plants that were used to make dyes and soap, fishing and the steady hunting of young Cory's shearwaters *(Calonectris diomedea borealis)*.

The Desertas are connected underwater to the Ponta de São Lourenço at a depth of one hundred and fifty metres.

In 1971 the islands were bought along with the Desertas by the Portuguese state, and later on transformed into a complete nature reserve.

An important protector of the Selvagens was Alec Zino, a conservationist and ornithologist, born in Madeira that gave his name to Zino's petrel, Europe's rarest breeding bird. After joining a scientific expedition to the Selvagens in 1963, Alec Zino bought the hunting rights for these islands to stop the annual hunting expeditions. For the following two decades and up to his death in 2004 Zino helped to protect and study the bird colonies, building the first house on the Selvagem Grande for this purpose.

The Selvagens are now widely recognized as a vital nesting sanctuary for sea birds, with the Cory's Shearwater colony counting fourteen thousand couples, and the white-faced-storm-petrels numbering over forty thousand couples. Apart from these there are seven other species of sea birds, a gecko, and a lizard.

The vegetation on Selvagem Pequena and Ilheu de Fora are intact - without ever having suffered the presence of man or introduced animals, making them specially interesting from a botanical point of view. In all there are eleven plants exclusive to the Selvagens.

The Selvagens have been linked to a long lost treasure, hidden there in 1701 by Captain Kidd, the Scottish pirate who attacked a Spanish galleon filled with the riches of the cathedral in Lima, Peru. During the nineteenth century at least four expeditions tried to find the treasure. In 1923, the English explorer Sir Ernest Shackleton came to Funchal claiming to have information from the naval ministry on where the treasure was hidden. He asked the owner of the Selvagens, Luis Rocha Machado, permission to look for the treasure on his way back from the South Pole. Unfortunately he died during his expedition and whatever information he had was lost with him. Nowadays most expeditions to the Selvagens are scientific, investigating the islands unique botany, wildlife, and geology.

The Selvagens are said to hide a fabulous treasure buried there by Captain Kidd in 1701.

Visitor's Guide

The addresses featured here, mostly refer to places mentioned in the book, or illustrated in the photographs. It is impossible to mention all of Madeira's good hotels, restaurants, gardens or places – but for more information on these contact the Madeira Tourism Board: Av. Arriaga 18, 9004-519 Funchal. Tel: + 351 291 211900. www.madeiratourism.org

Funchal

Where to Stay

THE CLIFF BAY *****
Estrada Monumental, 147, 9004-532 Funchal
Tel: +351 291 70 77 07
www.portobay.com
This excellent five star hotel is renowned for the quality of its service and cuisine. Luxurious gardens complement the breathtaking views, with great sea access and pool area.

REID'S PALACE HOTEL *****
Estrada Monumental, 9000-098 Funchal
Tel: +351 291 71 71 71
www.reidspalace.orient-express.com. Every moment of a stay in this splendid masterpiece is an unforgettable experience of luxury and good taste. The gardens and afternoon tea alone are worth the visit.

CASA VELHA DO PALHEIRO *****
Palheiro Golf, 9050, Funchal
Tel: +351 291 79 49 01
www.casa-velha.com
This Relais & Chateaux country house hotel sums up Madeira's charms with a fabulous historical garden in the property, golf course, and delicious food.

CHOUPANA HILLS RESORT & SPA *****
Travessa do Largo da Choupana, 9050-286, Funchal
Tel: +351 291 20 60 20
www.choupanahills.com
Surrounded by woods and just near the Levada dos Tornos, this hotel is set in the hills overlooking Funchal, were tranquillity reins. Luxurious stone and wood bungalows on stilts offer an exotic stay.

VILA PORTO MARE ****
R. Simplicio Passos de Gouveia, nº 21, 9004-565 Funchal
Tel: +351 291 70 37 00
www.portobay.com
The newest four star hotel in Madeira, which could easily be classified as a five star. With a diverse choice of restaurants, Spa, pools, sports facilities and superb service.

HOTEL PORTO SANTA MARIA ****
Av. Do Mar, 9050-029, Funchal
Tel: +351 291 20 67 00
www.portobay.com
Set in the heart of the old town and just in front of the sea, this hotel offers excellent service in a unique location.

QUINTA DA PENHA DE FRANÇA ****
R. Penha de França, 9000-014 Funchal
Tel: +351 291 20 46 50
www.hotelquintapenhafranca.com Charming traditional Madeiran quinta in a good location, with sea access, charming staff and excellent food.

Restaurants

IL GALLO D' ORO
The Cliff Bay
Estrada Monumental, 147, 9004-532 Funchal
Tel: +351 291 70 77 07
Regarded as one of Madeira's finest restaurants, Il Gallo d'Oro specializes in excellent Mediterranean food.

IL BASÍLICO
Vila Porto Mare
R. Simplício Passos de Gouveia, nº 21, 9004-565 Funchal
Tel: +351 291 70 37 00
This popular restaurant offers delicious no-fuss Italian dishes, with a local twist.

MED
Vila Porto Mare
R. Simplício Passos de Gouveia, nº 21, 9004-565 Funchal
Tel: +351 291 70 37 00
With an intimate atmosphere and fresh decoration, the chefs scabbard fish risotto is sublime.

JOE'S BAR RESTAURANT
R. Penha de França, 9000-014 Funchal
Tel: +351 291 20 46 50
This is a Funchal institution that serves very good Madeiran and Portuguese dishes.

VILA CIPRIANI
Estrada Monumental 139, Funchal
Tel: +351 291 71 71 00
With a sweeping terrace view of Reid's hotel and the sea, this restaurant serves fine Italian food in style.

CASA VELHA DO PALHEIRO
Palheiro Golf, 9050, Funchal
Tel: +351 291 79 49 01
Delicious gourmet dining in this traditional Relais & Chateaux country house hotel.

Pastry Shops

FABRICA STO. ANTONIO
Travessa do Forno 25-31, Funchal
Tel: +351 291 22 02 55
The delicious specialities include broas de mel, bolos de mel, and delightful tropical jams and ices.

PASTELARIA LUA
R. Carreira 78, Funchal
Tel: +351 291 22 07 70
Founded in 1845 this pastry shop has very good cakes, such as the Bolo de Rei

Cafés

GOLDEN GATE CAFÉ
Av. Arriaga, 9000 Funchal
Tel: +351 291 23 43 83
Always in the centre of things, this landmark of Funchal has delicious bolo do caco sandwiches, and cakes.

APOLO
Opposite Sé Cathedral, Funchal
Tel: +351 291 22 00 99
This traditional café has always been a reference in Funchal.

Market

MERCADO DOS LAVRADORES
Tel: +351 291 21 40 80
Madeira's biggest market is open every day until 20.00 except on Sunday.
Fruit, vegetables, flowers, spices, plants, meat, fish are all on sale at this art deco market.

Wines

OLD BLANDY WINE LODGES
Av. Arriaga 22, Funchal
Tel: +351 291 74 01 10
Housing the most famous Ma-

deira wine names such as Blandy's, Leacock, Cossart Gordan and Miles in a former sixteenth century monastery. Includes a museum, wine shop and vintage tasting room.

DIOGOS
Av. Arriaga 48, Funchal
Tel: +351 291 23 33 57
Selling Barbeito Madeira wines as well as other good Portuguese wines in this central shop. Downstairs is a small Columbus collection belonging to the Diogos family.

Bars

CAFÉ DO TEATRO
Av. Arriaga, 9000 Funchal
Tel: +351 291 24 99 59
A strategic meeting point were most of Funchal stops for a coffee at some time or other during the day, and at night it's *the* trendy bar to go.

CAFÉ DO MUSEU
Praça do Município, 9000 Funchal
Tel: +351 291 28 11 21
Situated just under the Sacred Art Museum it is an excellent place for a snack during the day or a drink at night.

Casino

CASINO DA MADEIRA
Av. Infante, 9000 Funchal
Tel: +351 291 20 91 80
Designed by Oscar Neimeyer, the Casino da Madeira is a landmark in Funchal with plenty of music and entertainment.

Gardens

PALHEIRO GARDENS
Palheiro Ferreiro, 9050, Funchal
Tel: +351 291 79 49 01
The most famous of Madeira's gardens, a new tea house has added even more to the superb natural attractions.

QUINTA PALMEIRA
R. da Levada da Santa Luzia, 31-A, Funchal
Tel: +351 291 22 10 91
Exotic trees and plants thrive in this English garden, with a spectacular view over the harbour.

JARDIM BOTÂNICO
Caminho do Meio, 9050 Funchal
Tel: +351 291 21 12 00
Set in a perfect location for plants to grow, the garden shows Madeira's native plants together with exotic cacti, topiary and orchids.

MONTE PALACE TROPICAL GARDENS
Caminho do Monte 174, Funchal
Tel. +351 291 78 23 39
This lush garden is exploding with plants and trees of all sizes. The cycads are especially worth a visit.

JARDINS DO IMPERADOR
Caminho do Pico, 9050 Funchal
Tel. +351 291 78 04 60
Tranquillity reigns in this truly Madeiran quinta, were enormous trees from all around the world live side by side with native species.

Wickers

CAFÉ RELOGIO
Camacha, town square
Tel: +351 291 92 21 14
Right near the town square, this hectic shop has thousands of wicker objects for sale and the artisans can be seen weaving the baskets.

Museums

MUSEU DE ARTE SACRA
R. do Bispo 21, 9000 Funchal
Tel: +351 291 22 89 00
One of the finest collections in Portugal of late fifteenth century and sixteenth century Flemish art, bought at the height of the sugar trade.

MUSEU DE ARTE CONTEMPORÂNEA
R. Portão S. Tiago, 9050 Funchal
Tel: +351 291 21 33 40
Set in the Forte S. Tiago, the exhibitions focus on Portuguese contemporary artists, mainly from the 60's.

CASA-MUSEU FREDERICO DE FREITAS
Calçada de Santa Clara 7, 9000 Funchal
Tel: +351 291 22 05 78
A fine eclectic selection of furniture, prints and ceramics relating to Madeira, as well as a superb azulejo tile collection.

MUSEU QUINTA DAS CRUZES
Calçada do Pico 1, 9000 Funchal
Tel: +351 291 74 06 70
The collections include Portuguese and English furniture, gold and silver artefacts and fine architectural relics in the gardens.

UNIVERSO DAS MEMORIAS JOÃO CARLOS ABREU, Calçada do Pico 2, 9000 Funchal
Tel: +351 291 22 51 22
Containing several collections of paintings, furniture, horse sculptures, silver and much more all donated to the region by the Regional Culture Minister, João Carlos Abreu.

CENTRO DAS ARTES CASA DAS MUDAS
Vale de Amores, 9370-111 Calheta
Tel: +351 291 822808
Set in Calheta on the Western Coast, a 20min drive from Funchal. Features modern art from around the world.

Big Game Fishing

BALANCAL
Palheiro Golf, 9050 Funchal
Tel: +351 291 79 49 01
The perfect big game fishing boat and crew to charter, is also available for dolphin and whale watching.

Levada Walks

An absolute must is a walk along one of the fabulous levadas of Madeira. Contact the Madeira Tourism Board for more information, www.madeiratourism.org

Embroidery

BORDAL
R. Dr. Fernão Ornelas 77, 9050 Funchal
Tel: +351 291 22 29 65
www.bordal.com
One of the best producers and exporters of the delicate Madeira embroidery. The very finest linen and cotton fabrics are used to make unique tablecloths, curtains, bedspreads, baby clothes and more. In downtown Funchal there are several other embroidery workshops, specially near the market.

Around the island

Where to Stay

QUINTA DO ARCO DE S. JORGE
Arco S. Jorge, Santana
Tel: +351 291 57 02 50
www.quintadoarco.com
Staying here is an absolute must. With private bungalows and gardens that look onto an impressive wall of green mountains. The gardens have over 17 000 roses to admire.

QUINTA DAS VINHAS
Sitio do lombo dos Serrões, 9370 Calheta
Tel: +351 291 82 00 40
www.qdvmadeira.com
This seventeenth century quinta has been faithfully restored, surrounded by vineyards and with sea views it is a superb alternative to staying in Funchal.

ESTALAGEM SERRA GOLF
Casais Proximos, Santo da Serra
Tel: +351 291 22 26 67
Just near the Santo da Serra golf course this charming hotel offers good service and great food.

ESTALAGEM DA PONTA DO SOL
Qta. da Rochinha, Ponta do Sol
Tel: +351 291 97 02 00
www.pontadosol.com
A member of the Design Hotels, this modern hotel is an unexpected sight in the traditional village of Ponta do Sol.

QUINTA DO FURÃO
Achada do Gramacho, 9230 Santana
Tel: +351 291 57 01 00
www.quintadofurao.com
Surrounded by sea and vineyards this 43-bedroom hotel is a great place to relax and discover the north coast.

Restaurants

A ADEGA
R. Joaquim da Costa, 9325 Estreito da Camara de Lobos
Tel: +351 291 91 05 30
Espetada with a view – this is the ideal place to taste Madeira's great speciality the espetada. Also try the bolo do caco with garlic butter and fried maize.

FAJÃ DOS PADRES
Tel: +351 291 77 44 58
This secluded cove is only accessible by private boat, or down a tiny cliff-hugging elevator, but once there it is well worth the journey. The castanhetas and tuna are delicious and so is the pitanga cheesecake.

ABRIGO DO POISO
Poiso
Tel: +351 291 78 22 69
An excellent stopping place near Pico do Areeiro for a great espetada, or simply for a taste of the local poncha drink.

CHÃO DA RIBEIRA
Tel: +351 291 85 45 59
This restaurant is off the tourist trail that goes straight to Porto Moniz. The trout is fresh and the meat espetada very good.

BAR AMARELO
Caniçal
Tel. +351 291 96 17 98
Specializing in local fish and seafood, it's a good choice for this part of the island.

Golf

SANTO DA SERRA GOLF
Santo António da Serra, 9200 Machico
Tel: +351 291 55 01 00
www.santodaserragolf.com
Home of the Madeira Island Open each year, the course is ranked as one of the top 100 in Europe. The 27 holes are surrounded by mountain and sea views, and the practice areas are superb.

PALHEIRO GOLF
Sitio do Balancal, 9050 Funchal
Tel: +351 291 79 21 16
www.palheirogolf.com
This 18 hole championship course is set in a fabulous location in the hills surrounding Funchal. The clubhouse has a breathtaking view of the harbour and serves excellent food.

Porto Santo

Ferry

LOBO MARINHO
R. da Praia 6, 9000 Funchal
Tel: +351 291 21 03 00
www.portosantoline.pt
With daily crossings to and from Porto Santo, the luxurious new ferry from Porto Santo Line also has day trips to discover this enchanted island. Offering a cinema, games area, solarium, and plenty of relaxing space it's the perfect way to travel to Porto Santo.

Where to Stay

HOTEL TORRE PRAIA ****
R. Goulart Medeiros, 9400 Porto Santo
Tel: +351 291 98 04 50
www.portosantoline.pt
In a prime spot on the beach and near the city centre, this hotel has plenty of restaurants and a sports bar.

HOTEL LUA MAR ****
Cabeça da Ponta, 9400 Porto Santo
Tel: +351 291 98 41 21
www.portosantoline.pt
Set in a dream location right on the beach, this apart-hotel offers a relaxing stay with stunning views of turquoise sea and sandy beach.

HOTEL DO PORTO SANTO ****
Campo de Baixo, 9400-015 Porto Santo
Tel. +351 291 980140
www.hotelportosanto.com
Comfortable hotel in a spectacular secluded location right on the beach.

Restaurants

PIZZA N'AREIA
Praia da Fontinha, Porto Santo
Tel. +351 291 98 04 57
A casual beach restaurant serving delicious pizzas and natural juices, right on the seafront.

O CALHETAS
Ponta da Calheta, Porto Santo
Tel: +351 291 98 43 80
The feijoada de gambas, and açorda de mariscos are legendary here; the food specializes in fish and seafood, which is natural as it is just on the Calheta beach.

TIA MARIA
Ribeiro Salgado, 9400 Porto Santo
Tel: +351 291 98 24 00
Serving traditional snacks such as *picadinho* and boiled shrimp in a dream location.

Torres
Sítio da Camacha,
9400 Porto Santo
Tel: +351 291 98 43 73
Locals know this as the best place to eat octopus starters and roast chicken.

La Roca
Clube Naval do Porto Santo
Porto de Abrigo,
9400 Porto Santo
Tel: +351 291 98 23 53
Open in the summer months only, the restaurant serves great caipirinha drinks and specializes in South American barbecued steaks.

Ice-Creams

Lambecas
Largo do Pelourinho, Vila Baleira
Founded forty-three years ago, the ice cream machine is still the same and producing the most deliciously refreshing ices.

Golf

Porto Santo Golf
The brand new golf course could not be in a more dramatic and beautiful setting, designed by golf champion Seve Ballesteros it will eventually have 45 holes.
For more information please contact the Madeira Tourism Board, www.madeiratourism.org

Horse-Riding

Campo da Barca
Porto Santo
Tel: +351 291 98 31 07
What better way to discover the island, than riding on interesting off road paths with excellent company.

Museums

Casa Museu Colombo
Travessa da Sacristia 2-4,
Vila Baleira
Tel: +351 291 98 34 05
The Christopher Columbus House is a place to visit in Vila Baleira, the original cereal storage pits found here are very interesting.

Tallasotherapy

Tallasotherapy
Sitio do Cabeço do Ponta,
9400 Porto Santo
Tel: +351 291 98 08 90
Offering various treatments with the local sands and water, massages and well-being exercises.

Nightlife

Penedo do Sono
A row of trendy bars and lively cafés look out onto the marina, with live music playing well into the night.
For more information please contact the Madeira Tourism Board, www.madeiratourism.org

Festivals & Events

February

Carnival
All of Funchal gets dressed up for Carnival, thousands of participants in street parades dancing to the sound of drums and music. The main parade takes place on Saturday, and the following Tuesday is a free-style costume parade.

March

Madeira Island Open
Held at the Santo da Serra Golf each year and part of the PGA European Tour. It always pulls in leading pros and guarantees spectacular golf watching.

April

Flower Festival
Each year this festival grows larger, with more street parades, dancing, flower carpets lining the streets and decorations all over Funchal.

June

Cherry Festival
Held in Jardim da Serra, the largest cherry-producing region on the island this event is celebrated with outdoor food stalls and live music.

Festival do Atlântico
Every weekend throughout June sees a series of concerts and fireworks with synchronized music dazzling the crowds in Funchal.

Festa de São João
This hails the beginning of summer in Porto Santo, with lots of entertainment and live music.

July

Funchal Jazz
One of the best events on the island, held in the gardens of the Quinta Magnolia in Funchal, it never fails to bring in great legends and rising jazz stars.

August

Rali da Madeira
This rally is part of the European championship, and offers the drivers and spectators a thrilling race through the mountains of Madeira.

Porto Santo Regatta
This yearly boat race from Funchal to Porto Santo and back is fiercely competitive and great fun.

September

Wine Festival
Held at the beginning of the month, the festival starts with grape picking in Câmara de Lobos. The celebrations are held throughout the island always accompanied to music and lots of wine crushing and tasting.

Columbus Week
During the last week of September various processions, live music and entertainment celabrate the life and achievements of the Genovese explorer.

December

Christmas & New Years' Celebrations Starting on the 8th December and going right through to the 6th January, Madeira is electric with Christmas lights and street music. The famous fireworks are held at midnight on New Year's Eve and fifty fireposts bring Funchal's amphitheatre to life.

Bibliography

Aragão, A, *A Madeira Vista por Estrangeiros*, Funchal, 1981.

As Ilhas Selvagens, ed. Região Autónoma da Madeira, Funchal, Secretaria Regional do Ambiente e dos Recursos Naturais, Serviço do Parque Natural da Madeira, 2003.

Binney, Marcus, *Country Manors of Portugal*, Lisbon, Difel, 1987.

Bowe, Patrick, *Gardens of Portugal*, Lisbon, Quetzal, 1989.

Boxer, C. R., *The Portuguese Seaborne Empire 1415-1825*, London, Hutchinson, 1977.

Bridge, Ann / Lowndes, Susan, *The Selective Traveller in Portugal*, London, Evan Brothers, 1949.

Cann, John P., *The Madeira Heritage in Colonial America*, pp.77-84, Lisbon, The British Historical Society of Portugal, 2003.

Camara, Duarte B., *Guia de Campo das Aves do Parque Ecologico do Funchal e do Arquipelago da Madeira*, Funchal, ed. Associação dos Amigos do Parque Ecológico, 1997.

Cane, Florence du, *The Flowers and Gardens of Madeira*, London, Adam and Charles Black, 1909.

Carita, Rui, *Historia da Madeira vols.I-IV*, Funchal, ed. Secretaria Regional da Educação, Juventude e Emprego, 1992.

Clode, Luiza / Helena e Aragão / José Victor, *Madeira*, Lisboa, Editorial Presença, 1989.

Cossart, N., *Madeira the Island Vineyard*, London, Christie's Wine Publications, 1984.

Costa Neves, Henrique, *Laurissilva da Madeira, Caracterização Quantitativa e Qualitativa*, Funchal, ed. Governo Regional, Secretaria Regional da Agricultura, Florestas e Pescas, Parque Natural da Madeira, 1996.

Farrow, John and Susan, *Madeira the Complete Guide*, London, Robert Hale, 1994.

França, Isabella de, *Journal of a Visit to Madeira and Portugal* (1853-1854), Funchal, ed. Junta Geral do Distrito Autonómo do Funchal, 1970.

Franquinho, L.O. e Costa, A., *Madeira, Plantas e Flores*, Funchal, ed. Francisco Ribeiro e Filhos, 1999.

Freitas, Paulo de, *'Casinhas de Prazer'*, Funchal, Revista Islenha, n.º8, Janeiro/ Junho 1991.

Frutuoso, G., *Livro Segundo das Saudades da Terra*, Ponta Delgada, 1968.

Funchal, Roteiro Histórico e Cultural da Cidade, Funchal, ed. Camara Municipal do Funchal, 1997

Gregory, Desmond, *The Beneficent Usurpers*, London, Associated University Presses, 1988.

Jardim, R. / Francisco, D., *Flora Endémica da Madeira*, Funchal, Múchia Publicações, 2000.

Johnson, Hugh, *The World Atlas of Wine*, 3rd Edition, London, Mitchell Beazeley Publishers, 1987.

Lacerda, Francisco de, *Folclore da Madeira e Porto Santo*, Lisboa, Edições Colbri, 1994.

Lethbridge, Alan, *Madeira: Impressions and Associations*, London, Methuen, 1924.

Liddell, Alex, *Madeira*, London, Faber and Faber, 1998.

Marques, Luiz, *The Anglo-Portuguese News – Special Madeira Number*, Lisbon 1969.

Mayson, Richard, *Portugal's Wines and Wine Makers*, London, Ebury Press, 1992.

Melo, Luís de Sousa / Farrow, Susan, *Impressões da Madeira Antiga*, Funchal, Livraria Inglesa, 1983.

Mestre, Victor, *Arquitectura Popular da Madeira*, Lisboa, Argumentum, 2002.

Monumentos Nº19, *Sé do Funchal*, Lisboa, ed. Direcção-Geral dos Edifícios e Monumentos Nacionais, 2003.

Museu de Arte Sacra do Funchal, Arte Flamenga, Museus da Madeira, texto de Luiza Clode, Lisboa, Edicarte, 1997.

Oliveira Marques, A. H., *História de Portugal*, 13ºed. , 3 vol., Editorial Presença, 1997-98, Lisboa.

Quest-Ritson, Charles, *The English Garden Abroad*, London, Viking, 1992.

Quintal, Raimundo, *Madeira a Descoberta da Ilha de Carro e a Pé*, Funchal, ed. Associação de Amigos do Parque Ecológico do Funchal, 2003.

Pereira, Eduardo CN, *Ilhas de Zargo*, Funchal, 4ª ed Câmara Municipal do Funchal, vols I e II, 1989.

Prada, Susana, *Geologia e Recursos Hídricos Subterrâneos da Ilha da Madeira*, Funchal, Universidade da Madeira, 2000.

Press, JP / Short, MJ, *Flora of Madeira*, HMSO, Natural History Museum.

Silva, João B. P. *Areia de Praia da Ilha do Porto Santo*, Funchal, Ed. Madeira Rochas, Divulgações Cientificas e Culturais, 2003.

Sitwell, Sacheverell, *Portugal and Madeira*, London, B. T. Batsford, 1954.

Stevenson, Tom, *The New Sotheby's Wine Encyclopedia*, London, Dorling Kindersley, 1997.

Vicente, Ana, *As Mulheres Portuguesas Vistas por Viajantes Estrangeiros*, Lisboa, Gotica, 2001.

Vieira, Alberto, *A Vinha e o Vinho na Historia da Madeira - Séculos XV-XX*, Funchal, ed. Centro de Estudos de História do Atlântico, 2003.

Walker, Carolyn, *The Embroidery of Madeira*, New York, Union Square Art Book, 1987.

Index

BANCO ESPÍRITO SANTO
Sucursal Financeira Exterior – Madeira Branch

CÂMARA MUNICIPAL
DO FUNCHAL

JERÓNIMO MARTINS

PORTO BAY HOTELS & RESORTS

SECRETARIA REGIONAL
DO TURISMO E CULTURA
Direcção Regional de Assuntos Culturais

SECRETARIA REGIONAL
DO TURISMO E CULTURA
Direcção Regional do Turismo

TECNOROCHA
GrupoTâmega

ACKNOWLEDGEMENTS

My sincere gratitude goes to the sponsors of this book who had the vision and generosity to support the project when it was just an abstract scheme, making it a reality.

I would like to thank Dr. Bruno Pereira and D. Maria Luisa Perestrello from the Madeira Tourism Office who were the first to jump on board, and a source of constant support. Eng. José Fonseca from Tecnorocha – Grupo Tamega helped me when I need it most, right at the beginning. Dr. Claudio Santos from Porto Bay Hotels & Resorts was a source of constant enthusiasm. Dr. Miguel Albuquerque, Mayor of Funchal was vital in keeping the project afloat, as was Escultor Ricardo Velosa from the Direcção Regional de Assuntos Culturais. Sr. João Alexandre Silva from Banco Espírito Santo SFE-Madeira and Dr. José Antonio Nogueira de Brito from Jerónimo Martins ensured the book maintained a high quality level throughout.

I would also like to thank my husband, Ricardo Abreu for his tireless campaigning and support. Jane Manaster for editing the text so beautifully. Antonia Leitão, Federica Leitão and Sofia Leitão for their constant creative input and help in all stages of this book.

Lastly, and most importantly, I would like to thank Alma E. Mollemans for being the perfect photographer and partner for this book, adopting it as his own, and Ben Santo for bringing such an elegant design to our ideas as well as giving the book its own personality and life.

Concept, Writing and Translation
CRISTINA LEITÃO

Photography
ALMA E. MOLLEMANS

Design
BEN SANTO

Editing
JANE MANASTER

Production Coordinator
FEDERICA LEITÃO

Second Edition 2005
First published 2004

C. A. LEITÃO PUBLICATIONS
MADEIRA

WWW.CALEITAO.COM
cristinaleitao@netmadeira.com

Depósito Legal 215799/04
ISBN 972-9060-42-8
Printed and bound in Portugal by PRINTER PORTUGUESA

for AMELIE